QUEEN OF THE ROAD

Poetry of the Goddess Aset

BY CHELSEA LUELLON BOLTON

Lulu Press, 2016

Queen of the Road: Poetry of the Goddess Aset

Printed in the United States of America
First Printing, 2016
ISBN: 9781796836578
http://fiercelybrightone.com

Dedication

This work is of course dedicated to Aset.

I would like to also thank my family for supporting me during the making of this project. Thank you especially to Mom, Dad, Jeremy and Ami.

Table of Contents

Part III: The Ancestral Goddess

Part IV: Magic of the Goddess

Part V: Attributes of the Goddess

Part VI: Family of the Goddess

Part VII: Festivals of the Goddess

Part VIII: To the People of the Goddess

Part IX: Priesthood of the Goddess

Part X: The Goddess's Husband Wesir (Osiris)

Part XI: Songs of the Goddess

Part XII: Epilogue

Acknowledgements

Thank you to Tamara L. Siuda.

Thank you to Kiya Nicoll, T. Thorn Coyle and Lady Olivia Robertson.

Thank you to my family, especially Mom, Jeremy, Ami and Dad.

Thank you to Christie B. Tina K., Nikki and Liza M. for their continued friendship and support throughout this project.

Thank you to all of the Egyptologists who worked so hard to make the information about Aset available to all.

Introduction

Here is a collection of poetry exploring the many aspects of the ancient Egyptian Goddess Aset, more commonly known as Isis.

Within these poems, She is described as the Goddess of the stars at night, the celestial bodies above, and the sunrise. She is the Goddess of the inundation of the Nile, the crops and plants which flourish by the riverbanks and the sun which warms and scorches the Earth. She is the wind and rain Goddess. She is the Star Goddess. She is the Lady of Rivers and Streams.

She is the Goddess of Life-Power, which includes the ancestral and magical powers of creation. She is a magician, a sorceress and a healer. She is a mourner and caretaker of the dead. She is a Powerful Goddess who knows the Name which created the Universe.

She is not alone in the Universe. She has a family of Gods and Goddesses with Her, including Her parents, siblings, husband, partners and children. Some of the poems delve a little deeper into these relationships as both members of a family and forces which create and maintain the cycles of the cosmos.

There are poems which explore Her many celebrations such as the festivals, feasts and processions of the Goddess. Some festivals explored in the poems are the Rhodophoria, Aset Luminous and Her Navigation festivals. These poems explore the myths or the celestial, earthly or ethereal cycles associated with each festival.

Other poems explore messages and advice for the modern devotees and/or priests on which one may ponder.

This poetry is inspired by the Goddess and is not a substitute for any legal, medicinal or spiritual advice or services. If you are in dire straits, please get the services you need from a competent professional.

In order to fully appreciate these poems, it would help the reader to be familiar with Egyptian Mythology, especially Aset's myths, and some ancient Egyptian concepts such as the *Ka* or the vital essence of a being. The *ka* is the vital essence or life-force portion of the soul that we inherit through our ancestors all the way back to the Creator. Every living thing from Gods, humans, animals and nature have *kau.*[1] This is also the same energy that makes up *hekau* or magic. Some resources about these topics are listed in the bibliography.

The Goddess within these poems is the Ancient Egyptian Goddess Aset rather than Isis, the Greco-Roman Goddess of the Classical World.

Aset is a Goddess of sovereignty, kingship, ancestral lineage and traditions, death, magic, healing, protection, and knowledge. She is the throne of kings, a Goddess who governs over the authority of rulers and the sovereignty of kings. She is the faithful wife, who stayed married to Her husband even after his death. She is a devoted mother, who raised her son, protecting him from dangerous forces and assisted him throughout his trials for Kingship. She is a trickster, using her guile to obtain the power of Ra's Name. She is a powerful sorceress, who halted the Sun Boat in order to heal Her son and who conceived an heir from Her dead husband. She is a compassionate healer, who cured a boy from a scorpion sting despite the transgressions of his mother. She is the Great of Magic, all magic and knowledge are Hers to command for she knows all in Heaven and on Earth.

She is a cunning shape-shifter, a wily trickster, a powerful sorceress and a devoted wife and mother in the myths. She mourned Her slain husband and raised her son alone. She is the protector of Her brother, son and father.

She is the star Sopdet (Sirius) who heralded the Nile's flood, the New Year and the calculation of festival calendar. She is the Goddess of every year and of sacred time. She is both a beneficial Goddess of rainfall and the

1   Bell, Lanny. "The New Kingdom Divine Temple: The Example of Luxor," in Temples of Ancient Egypt, ed. Byron E. Shafer, (New York: Cornell University Press, 1997), 131-132 and 140.

terrifying Goddess of the torrential flood. As a protective Eye of Ra, She's the Goddess of the warmth of the sun and its scorching, fiery rays. Blue is the color of the fiercest fire and white is the brightest of lights; these are Her colors which aptly describe Her nature for She is both a fierce and bright Goddess.[2]

Hopefully, these verses will give you some glimpse into the nature of Aset and the other Egyptian Gods associated with Her. May Her mysteries be revealed, Her aspects be known, and Her messages be heard.

May these poems enrich your life.

Best Regards,
Chelsea Bolton

---

2   [2] Bolton, Chelsea Luellon. <u>Lady of Praise, Lady of Power: Ancient Hymns of the Goddess Aset</u>. (Lulu Press, 2016), VI.

PART I

Devotion to the Goddess

Awaken

Cool crisp breeze
Creeps across the sand
Glimmer of Light
Peaks out
On the Horizon
A woman clothed in white
Offers *Henu* to Your Shrine
Food is given to Your Image
Water is poured on Your Holy Ground
People rejoice in Your House
A new day Becomes
And You Awaken

Awake in Peace, O Aset

Awake in Peace, O Goddess of Beauty
Awake in Peace, O Goddess of Life's joy
Mother Aset, awaken and come to life
You who are the Mother of all Mothers
The Goddess of all Goddesses
You who fill the river banks with your tears
For Your Husband slain
You who gave birth from death
Mistress of Creation
Owner of Ra's Name
Great of Magic, Mistress of *Heka*
Death's Mourner
Inertia's Bride
You who bend possibility to Your will
Awaken peacefully on this day

Holy Aset

Dua Aset
Henu
My body and spirit cleansed for You
As I enter Your Temple
Open the holy Naos
Gaze upon Your Image
In adoration
In awe
Of All You Are
I worship You
I bow before You
I pledge my life to You
Most Glorious Goddess

Temple of Aset

I come in service of the King
I come in service of the Goddess
I come in service of the God
I come in service of the People
I come in service of the Nation
I come in service of the Lady of Flame, the Lady of Incense
I come in service of the Lord of Grain--Her Husband
I come in service of the Goddess of All Goddesses,
the Mistress of *Heka*
Aset,
The Goddess who sees the enemies fall
Lady of the Lake, Lady of the Nile
Lady of the Waters of Life
Come to Your image, Your Seat, Your resting place
Come sit upon Your Throne
Adorned with Jewels

Queen

Queenship
Mut, the Vulture
Bird of Prey
Protector of Her flock
Eater of the Dead
Devourer of the Wicked
Obliteration of Fear
You protect me
You encircle me
Watching~
Swooping down~
Grazing me with Your talons
Blood trickles from my veins
Hardship makes me stronger
Landing on my arms
Gripping me with Your claws
Guidance of my Being
Maker of my Ka
Possessor of my True Self
I follow You into the depths of the damned
I am made whole
Burning in Your light
Transformed
Restored
Renewed

My Lady
My Mother
My Queen

Mut *here could mean "Mother". The vulture was one of Aset's sacred animals and other birds of prey as well such as the kite and the falcon. Just food for thought.*

Aset's Child

Push forth
O Aset
Birth Your son
Legs outstretched
Life comes out from Your womb
Heir to Your beloved throne
Lady of righteous indignation
Power of authority
Mother of Heru
Queen
Hold Your child
Close to Your breast
Nurse and care for Him
Teach Him Your wisdom
Guide Him
As You guide all Your Children

Fear Lifted

Tumbling through the ocean
Diving deep
Touching sand
Obscure bottom
Filled with hidden knowledge
Experiencing affection with another
The face I see
Guiding me home
Is You
Barriers fade away

Pendant Winged

Clasped hand
Pendant, old and dear
Fire of the sun
Heka of the world
Protection of the dearest kind
Wings of clarity
Beat away the turbulence of fear
Uraeus of Ra
Aid me in fighting my demons
Red soaked with blood
My hands scream
Seared flesh can only mend so soon
Heart beating with no pulse
Bending
Henu, my Lady
My Mother
Resuscitate me
In Your healing
In Your Rays

Homecoming

The blood of Aset entwined with my own
Desert winds tear skin~piece by piece
Away from my bones
At rest in Her arms
Death take me home

(Note: I wrote this after seeing Her and myself in the desert in front of a pyramid. Both of us were bleeding on the cheek. Then the winds picked up and cyclone around me. All that was left of me was a skeleton. Then She comes over and wraps Her arms around me.)

Bird of Prey

I made you
You are Loved
As the Bird of Prey
Sweeps down
And catches you
In My talons
Swooping you up to the Heavens
Never letting you
Tread upon the Earth
Ascended
Forever with Me

I am There

Be in love with who you are
For I made you that way
With your Beloveds

Who fastened you from clay
My breath flows through your veins
My essence is in your soul

I am there, My child.
I am within you, and without.
I am intertwined with every facet of your Being,
with every facet of this world.

I am there.

Look for Me.
You will find Me
In Wings' shadows
Gliding on a breath of air
in the Sunlight.

Name

What is the Work of this God?
How do I know myself if I don't know my own name?
If I don't know my own voice
How will I hear the inner silence?
How will I hear myself speak?
Distractions are all around me.
From TV shows, to books, the news,
My parents
Society as a Whole
Who am I?
What is my Work?
What is the Work for this God, my Lady?
What is my Work for Aset?
How will I know what love is
If I don't know my own name?
How will I hear my heart beat
If my insides are numb?
Chilled to the bone
How can my *ka* be fed
With love, life and laughter
If my *ka*,
Cannot flow from my heart?
How do I know my own name?
If no one speaks
If I don't speak
Or know
The name

Upon which the Gods gave me
The name
Upon which I was born
My Ren
Where is my identity?
What is my identity?
Why was I created?
How do I move through the world?
How do I know myself
if I don't know my own name?
Aset, My Mother
You have all of Me as your Mother
I am Aset for you
I am your Mother in every manifestation I possess
The closest one facet to you
is Aset of the West
This can be Aset Amenti
This can be Aset-Nebet Het
And this can be Aset-Nut
I am Aset-Nut first for you because of the work you do and will do for
Me
I am Aset-Tayet, when you need cleanliness and purity
I am Aset-Sekhmet for you when you need fierce love
I am Aset-Iryt Ra (Eye of Ra) for you when you need the power of
destructive fire to cleanse away entropy
I am Aset-Weret Hekau, as the Great Magician for you when you
need the power of My speech to make changes in your life and within
yourself
I am Aset-Serqet for you when you need to expel poisons
I am Aset-Hethert for you
when you need all things Hethert would give
For I am your Hethert
I provide for you when you need love, creativity and joy

For I am the Mistress of these for you
I am the Goddess of the starry Heavens for I am Mehet Weret for you
I guide the floodwaters as Aset-Sopdet as the Star in Heaven
I renew land, water and sky
I am the Wife of Wesir Wennefer
I am the consort of Min
I am also His Mother
Heru-sa-Aset is My son
I am the consort of Wepwawet
I am His Mother
Yinepu is My Sister's son, yet I am also His Mother
As We are both Wives of Wesir
And I adopted Him
I am the consort of Sobek
I am also His Mother
I am Amenti for you
I am Aset-Nebet Het for you
I am Aset-Nut for you
As I walk between worlds
As you do and will do
For Me
As My Priestess

Daughter of Aset, the Lioness

I am the Lioness of My Mother
Lady, Fiercely Bright One
Sorceress, Magical Lady
Her Voice is as Powerful as a roar

What She says, comes to pass
Lady of Bewitching Eyes
Eloquence, Wit, Charm
Royalty,
Cunning,
Owner of Ra's Name
Weeping Goddess

I was numb, I wept for years
My heart filled with tears
overflowing like the Nile
Sorrow without end

Drowning in my anguish
Weeping as You did
Caught in a whirlpool
I was almost pulled in~then

You came
With strong arms, You pulled me up
Words flowed from Your lips
Words of wisdom and power

Banishing my fear and my regret
and then

Embers glowed in darkness
Fiercely Bright
as the flames shot forth
and my soul
was renewed

Tempered by Your Flame
and cleansed by Your water
Nestled in darkness
I am made new

I am a Daughter of Aset
Proud and strong,
fierce and cunning
cultivating wisdom
gaining Power
through knowledge
and reverence.

I am a Daughter of Aset
the Fiercely Bright One
the Lioness of the Sun
the Lady of Stars
May Her voice as Powerful as a roar
Be mine also
May Her strength as strong as any lioness
Be mine to wield
For am I not the Daughter of the Mistress of Magic?
Am I not the Daughter of the One Who Knows Ra's Name?
Is this not my Power also?

To wield with wisdom and grace, with fortitude and honor?

What I choose will come to pass because I choose it.
Her Power is my Power.
And I am never alone.

Where my Goddess Dwells

Where is my Goddess?
In Her Country
On Her Throne
Where is my Lady?
In Her Shrine, In Her Image
Where is my Lady?
In the Shining Sun and Starry Sky
She stands at the Gate to the Ancestors
She Guards Their Knowledge, Their Tradition
The flowing waters, the burning blaze
Destroyer and Life-Giver, She Ascends
Screeching hawk as it descends
Stinging scorpion buried under sand
Stampede, trampling the land, Cow Goddess
Stealthy hunter, Lioness Queen,
Wailing and Wielding a Blade
Fierce and Feral
Gentle and Kind
I am where my Goddess dwells

PART II

Aspects of the Goddess

Mother of Kings

I am the Mother of Kings
I am the Goddess of sovereignty
I place the king upon His seat
I place My son upon His throne
I place My daughter who becomes My son upon Her throne
I give them power
I give them might
I give them *heka* so nations can fall or rise at their command
So too can this power be yours
Or anyone's
Who does the work to have this power in themselves
The power of self-possession
Is the power of the soul
united in all its parts
united in all its goals
Something so deep-rooted and deep-seeded
That it cannot be shaken
The tree that grows despite adversity
is strong
Towering, reaching for the sky
Hundreds or thousands of years
The grass that bends in a hurricane
is strong
Feeding those who stand upon it
Strength of the earth in all its forms
Both of these must be utilized
in order to own yourself

And this is the power I bring
I am the Mother of Thrones
I place those upon their seat
Who can bare to look at their souls
Discard the parts that are no longer needed
Take an honest look at themselves
And heal despite the pain
And heal the sorrow of their souls
This is not an easy task
This takes years
And once the tears are dry
And once the wailing silenced
Only then can growth sprout from this death
The heart renews its birth
New life can forge itself from the old
And you are reborn
And this is the power I bring
the power to own yourself
In all ways, in all forms
So that you too may be self-possessed

Kingmaker

I am adorned as Aset
Seated Upon Her Throne
Her brow adorned with the cobra
The Diadem between His Eyes
Fierce Protector of His People
Ruler of the Country, Nation, Tribe
All look to beseech His guidance
For the Decision Maker must act alone
Counsels can only advise so far
And this is Her power
One in charge of many
By blood or vote
By God descent
The order is established
Order starts among the people
By the One Who Leads
This is the focal point
The king is a king because of His Mother
He cannot sit upon My Seat without My consent
For I am the Kingmaker

Authority

What is the essence of this Goddess?
She is authority,
Of the king and social order,
Of magic and healing,
Of the dead and their remembrance.
For She made kings of Ra and Wesir,
Enabling them to rule with Her power,
Through Her magic, She healed her son and raised Her husband
Repelling illness with words laced with flame
With Her tears, She made men mourn for the dead and the loss of
the bereaved
Sorrow Transformed.

Colors of Aset

I am Red as the Eye of Ra
I am White as the Magician and the Purifier
I am Blue as the Lady of Heaven and the Mourner
I am Green as the Lady of Crops and the Good Wife
Silver is the Moon of My Husband and Son
For I rejuvenated the Sound Eye
The Slain King I made whole again

Eye of Ra

I am the Eye of Ra
I am the coiling snake, the hissing serpent
I am the flame that scorches and burns

I am the Eye of Ra
I am the lioness, the leopard, the jaguar
I am the stealth of four paws, shifting to match my surroundings

I am the Eye of Ra
I am the hawk, the female falcon, the kite
I am the shrieking bird hovering above the corpse

I am the Eye of Ra
I am the Seat of Power of Rulers and Kings
I am the flame which scorches their enemies

I am the Eye of Ra
I am the Shrine, the doorway, the unseen
I am the Spirit manifesting in sacred space, in sacred time

I am the Eye of Ra
I am God Herself
I am the Goddess, Whole

Aset-Tayet, the Purifier
I am the Purifier
No one becomes a *Wab* or *Wabet*
But through Me
I am the purity
Of the Shrine
Of the Home
Of Yourself
Come to Me when you need to be cleansed
Of dirt and entropy
Of sorrow and pain
What you bring into Shrine
Comes to Me
So the heaviness of your heart
Or the joy in your soul
Are what you bring with you
Cry the tears of Nebet Het
Lament My tears for My slain husband
Rejoice in My finding Him
The renewal is the cycle of Wesir
As the moon waxes and wanes
As the waters flood and recede
As the natron is washed ashore and brought before Me
For I am the one that cries
For I am the one who renews
Bathe in natron water
Tears, the origin of humankind
Tears, sorrow and joy expressed by the human eye
All of this is cleansed
Before you enter My shrine
For I am the purity of Tayet
I am Aset, the Purifier

Mother of All

Bejeweled
I emerge
From the waters
Glistening in Starlight
I am the Star Goddess of creation
I am the blue-hued Cow
I am the Bovine Goddess
Mother of the Gods
Mother of the Goddesses
I am the Mother of All
I am the Lioness
I am the Spotted Leopard
I am the Feline of Stars
I am the Eye of Ra of the Night
I am the fires of starlight
For these are small suns
Burning
These are the lights of creation
This is the fire of the soul
The fire in the hearth
The fire in your heart
All comes from the *ka*
All comes from Me
The Mother
I bring life

I transform the dead
All come from Me
For I am the Mother of All

Aset-Mut

I am Aset-Mut
I am the Mistress of Crowns
I am the Goddess of kings
I am the Goddess of the renewal of the ancestors
I am the Goddess of the inheritance of the Kingly Ka
I am the Goddess who oversees the ka-spirit of families
And I renew creation this way
I am the Goddess of sovereignty
Kingly Power
Personal Power
are Mine to command
I am the Goddess who does not yield
I am the Goddess of queens
I am the Female Ruler
of tribe or nation
I am the One who bestows the office of the ancestors
Upon those who are worthy
And those that are not, I destroy
I am the one who is self-possessed
I own My power
I own My strength
I am the woman, I am the Goddess
who will not be ruled
For I rule Myself
I own My power
And I give it to no one
I share Myself with those whom I please

But My power, My strength is Mine
No one else's
And I am the Goddess who is Queen
I am the sorceress who will not be ruled

Aset-Hethert

You have the soul of an artist.
It does not matter what method you use to create art.
Creating art is what is important.
I am the Goddess of artists. Not just Hethert.
I can create joy as well as sorrow.
There is a reason why We are connected.
There is a reason why We are syncretized.
We join when We must.
We join when emotion and art coalesce,
when passion meets determination,
when art has a goal and a purpose.
We join.
We are the Goddesses of gemstones hidden in the earth,
in Our Father and My Husband.
We join when the bereaved come to the graves.
We weep with them, We mourn with them.
We help them remember their dead and feed their ka.
We are turquoise, We are malachite, We are lapis lazuli.
We are blue and green swirled together.
We are music written and sang,
We are dance, choreographed and spontaneous.
We are words in art, melody in music and notes plucked on strings.
We are the joy that comes from creation
and the avenging Goddess,
whose wrath must be appeased
when creation is defiled.
Was not creation defiled when My Husband was slain?

Was not creation defiled when humanity threatened Ra?

I am the avenging Goddess as the Mother of Heru-sa-Aset
and as the solar Eye, avenging Her Father.
I am Sekhmet-Mut.
I am Sekhmet as Queen.
I am the Solar Mother, the Wrathful Avenger.
I am the Sole Eye of creation and death.
I am creation in the water and I am creation of the water.
The sky and primordial ocean are a part of Her,
just as they are apart of Me.
I am the Mother of the sun God,
She is the Mother of the sun God.
We are His daughters.
I am the star that rises and brings the flood.
She is the star that rises. I renew Wesir. She does also.
I renew Hethert. She renews Me.
We are the Ladies of the Stars.
The night sky is Our embrace.
I am the Queen of the Sistrum, the Queen of the Dance.
Life comes from Me, and death also comes to Me.
I am the narrow passage between worlds.
I am Aset.
I am Hethert.
We are One.
We are the light of the soul
and the place where people come to rest.
In Our embrace is the process of renewal.
This is where We meet.
All come to rest in Me.

Aset-Nut, the Lady of Heaven

I am Aset-Nut
I am together with My Mother
We are One
Both of Us are present
I give birth to My Mother and She gives birth to Me
I am contained within My Mother
She is contained within Me
For I have inherited
What is in My Mother
I am the Sovereign of the Sky,
The Lady of Heaven,
Mistress of the Stars
The Pot that pours the rain
The tears which overflow
The Cow that births the sun and stars
I am the Lady of the Night
The starry Heavens are My Domain
Because of My Mother
For I am with Her
We are One
I am Aset within Nut
I am Nut within Aset
And She is within Me
What I have
I have gotten from My Mother
She and I are One
We build and transform

Look to the Sky
We are there
As Many and as One

Aset-Nut, the Mother of Stars

I am your Mother in this tradition
Where are My jars of natron?
Where are My pools of water?
To bathe in?
To cleanse in?
I am the night sky
I am the ancestress of all of creation
Where is My *ka*?
Where is My *ba*?
Where does My power manifest?
I am the Mother of Stars
I am the Star Goddess
I renew ancestors and Gods
I pass down the *ka*
To families and kings
Because I am the Mother of All
All who weep
All who mourn
Are renewed through Me
All who honor their dead kin
Are renewed through Me
For I am the Mother of the Dead
For I am the Mother of the Stars
I am the Mother of the Living
I am the birth of Wesir and His death
Because I am with Nut
And She is His Mother

And She is His final resting place
For when We are One
I am His Mother
His Wife
His Mourner
It is My realm in which He rests
It is My realm in which He is transformed
From birth until death
And beyond
For there is life in the Otherworld
And I am its caretaker
I am the Mother of both living and dead
And I am the Goddess of the ancestral stars
The ancestral mothers
Who give birth and watch over their kin
And these ancestors call out to You
Because you will listen
Because you will do what they ask
You help your family in more ways than you realize
Their *ka* is cleansed
They are renewed
They are renewed
They are renewed
Through Me
Through You
Because I am the Star Goddess

Aset-Nut, the Devouring Flame

I am the Goddess Who Devours
I am the Goddess of the Red Cloth
I am the Veiled Lady of Stars
All who wish to be transformed
Come through My gates
Travel through My caverns
All who leave are irrevocably changed
For I am the Goddess of transformation
I am the Goddess of the night
I am the blue sky and the dark cavern
I am the transformation of the dead
And the renewal of the living
And I am the Devouring Goddess
Nothing that is against Ma'at may pass My gate
My mouth opens and swallows
Stagnation falls away
Burning embers destroy what cannot be sustained
Decay and self-betrayal
Self-loathing and lies
Are destroyed by My flame
So that the *ka* may be renewed
Transformed
Into something better
More stable than it was
Nothing can withstand this fire
Nothing can withstand this flame
For it is the essence of blue fire

It is the ka-force that must be maintained
It must change
Or it too will stagnate
Life cannot come from energy that does not change
What stagnates, dies
And then transforms into something new
But death is very permanent
One cannot be what one was
One must change
One must be transformed
With the fire
Of Nut
Of Aset
In order to be transformed
In order to be cleansed
One must walk through the fires of transformation
Ordeal
I am Aset-Nut
When I am the hippopotamus
When I am the leopard
When I am the Celestial Cow
Yet I can be these Myself as well
She is added for a specific function
As the Devourer of Souls
As the Mother of the Dead
As the Mistress of Stars
I am Aset-Nut for you when you need these things
And this is the Aset closest to you
In certain circumstances
But I am Aset for you
First
And I am Aset-Sekhmet

Second
For I am the lioness
I am the Avenger
I am the Goddess wielding a scimitar
With blood-filled rage
Who avenged My husband
My son and I
He did not do this alone
I was with Him through the entire ordeal
And it was an Ordeal
It is the transformation all
Spirit-Workers go through
All Shamans
All Mystics
All Priests
All Priestesses
It is the transformation of the Self
From a broken individual
To someone who walks in their own power
To someone who owns themselves
Self-Possession is not for the weak
You must wrestle with your demons
You must be exposed, vulnerable, bare
Naked to yourself
And see yourself for all you are
Both good and bad
Both pleasant and reviled
The Magician must do this as well
In order to be effective
This is why the migration of the soul
Is so important
It is not just a journey through a maze
But one of transformation

From one state of being to the next
The you before is not the you now
You are forever changed
This shift in self
Is an energetic current
It is a part of your soul
That shifts, moves and transforms
All the parts are affected
The *ka* is cleansed and shifts
The heart is unburdened and shifts
The *Ba* is cleaned and becomes whole
To feed your *ka* is to follow your heart
This is the center of your being
To cleanse your *ka* is to honor your ancestors
And to let go of what is no longer useful to you
What does not feed you?
Take it away
Cleanse it away
Transform it
So that it, in another form
May serve you better
Do this because
You want to
Not for any other reason
Not for Me
Not for your parents
Not for anyone else
This is for you
All of you
Because when you come to My Mother's Gate
You will be renewed again
And the journey is less painful to those
Who are masters of themselves

In whatever form that takes

For there are many ways for you to become truly who you are

Aset-Nut, the Divine Mother

I am the Divine Mother
I am the Lady of the House
I am the Lady of the Home
I am the Mistress of the Stars
I am the Divine Mother
I hold all in My embrace
In the Sky
And on the Earth
Heaven is My abode
Yet I am everywhere
I permeate everything
Because I am the Divine Mother
I gave birth to All
Even Ra
For I am His Mother
And He is My Son
I gave birth to the stars
The ancestors are My children
Their descendents are My offspring
And I am the Cow that adorns the sky
And I am the Leopard that devours
And all of Us are strewn with stars
Even the hippo.
The blue hippo
Are the waters of creation
Stars are but reflected light off the surface
Water glistening with life

Do you see?
Do you understand?
I am the Divine Mother
I gave birth to all
And what I gave birth to
I protect
I nurture
I bring power to those who are weak
I cause the suffering to endure
I am the sorrowful Mother
Raising Her son alone
I understand grief
I am the Wailing Woman
I am the Goddess who shrieks
I lost My love
This pain is ever-present
This pain is never ceasing
Yet, I continue
My son continues
And My husband is avenged
Yet I do not regain Him
As sons who have lost mothers
And daughters too
As mothers who have lost children
I understand
I renew
For pain can be transformed
A Mother's love never ends
Even in death
The dead feel their Mothers
The Mothers remember the dead
And the cycle continues
And sorrow turns into a dull ache

As time passes
Yet it never truly leaves
For just as becoming a Mother
Changed your soul
So too, does losing a son or daughter
And I am here
In this sorrow
In this pain
Holding you in My embrace
For I am the Divine Mother

Aset, My Mother

You have all of Me as your Mother
I am Aset for you
I am your Mother in every manifestation I possess
The closest one facet to you
is Aset of the West
This can be Aset Amenti
This can be Aset-Nebet Het
And this can be Aset-Nut
I am Aset-Nut first for you because of the work you do and will do for
Me
I am Aset-Tayet, when you need cleanliness and purity
I am Aset-Sekhmet for you when you need fierce love
I am Aset-Iryt Ra (Eye of Ra) for you when you need the power of
destructive fire to cleanse away entropy
I am Aset-Weret Hekau, as the Great Magician for you when you
need the power of My speech to make changes in your life and within
yourself
I am Aset-Serqet for you when you need to expel poisons
I am Aset-Hethert for you
when you need all things Hethert would give
For I am your Hethert
I provide for you when you need love, creativity and joy
For I am the Mistress of these for you
I am the goddess of the starry Heavens for I am Mehet Weret for you
I guide the floodwaters as Aset-Sopdet as the Star in Heaven
I renew land, water and sky
I am the Wife of Wesir Wennefer

I am the consort of Min
I am also His Mother
Heru-sa-Aset is My son
I am the consort of Wepwawet
I am His Mother
Yinepu is My Sister's son, yet I am also His Mother
As We are both Wives of Wesir
And I adopted Him
I am Amenti for you
I am Aset-Nebet Het for you
I am Aset-Nut for you
As I walk between worlds
As you do and will do
For Me
as My Priestess

Aset-Amenti, Lady of the West

The tide came in
And I say these words:
I will not yield.
Not one inch
Not one foot
I will not give way to the tide rolling in
of fear and turmoil
surging in its wake
I will shout across the shore
I will scream against the roar of crashing waves.
I will cry~rain will pour from my eyes
My tears themselves are a downpour
I will shriek~wind howling as it carries my voice
I will wail~keening the lament of a mourner.
Shaking, Trembling
Leaving hallowed husks in its wake
I am the Mourner of Souls
My voice carries a thousand screams in a whisper

I dare not weep
the keening of a mourner
I dare not cry for my tears will flood the oceans
and all shall perish in Her wake
I dare not wail
Only the deaf can hear my shrieking
Only torrents of rain can drown out my sorrow
Only thirst is My companion

as water falls from my eyes
I am air that has never lifted to the clouds
I am breath never spoken
I am words, never given a voice
I am the air of the ocean
Churning the sea
I am the Ocean's depths
I am Ocean's shore
I am the water on this primeval mound
I am the air of the darkened sky
I am the words first spoken
I am the voice first heard
The Creator calls and I am She
I am the One in the depths of the Waters
And I sing
And as I sing and as I speak, the waters churn
And creation bursts forth
All plants, all animals, all life
Rivers and oceans come from Me.
Mountains and lands of My Father
Land grows where My son and father walk.
For land is the lack of water
and water is the lack of land.
My Father knows and so do I
the ways of the ocean.
I am the Mother of Waters.
I am Nut, of the primeval mound.
I am Hethert, of the primeval mound.
I am Aset, of the primeval ocean.
I am the Cow Goddess here.
I am Lady Nebet Het as well.
For She Speaks Through Silence.
And We are all Ladies of the West.

This is Our Domain.
Creation and Death.
This is Who I am, child.
As your Mother.
I am All Mothers.
For I gave birth to all that exits.
And I am the Star Goddess of Heaven.
And I, and I alone
decide what exists.
My Father and brother beside Me.
I as I speak, waters churn.
Breath brings water to life.
And it is I,
not Hethert
Who brings this down.
She is joy.
and I am Silence.
I am Death.
I am words unspoken.
I am words, unneeded. The Message is clear.
When one dies, you need not speak.
You wail.
You scream.
You shout.
You cry.
Words flow in the sound of your voice.
This is the Power of Creation.
These are the words first spoken.
Oh, How beautiful to behold.
This life.
Look at its splendor.
Gaze as its beauty.
It is beauty born of silence.

I am Aset-Hethert.
I am Aset-Nebet Het.
I am Aset-Nut.
I am Aset, Lady of the West.
And I am the Cow Goddess here.
Lady of Silence.
This is My task.
Learn the Words of the Great Mother.
Love. Learn. Live.

And as I speak, the waters churn,
And as I speak, silence breaks
One voice
One word
No silence.
Light bursts forth.
One Dawn.
One Star
One Light.
I dispel darkness
I disperse light
All darkness falls before Me as I shine
As I burn, fire in darkness
Sunlight, Starlight
This is where I am.
And all evil trembles
when I speak
As I speak, water churns
As I burn, darkness hides
For this alone is where I reside

Appear as She Needs
I will appear as I need
to whomever calls to Me
You need Isis, if you honor Me in the classical way
if you need the Great Mother or Lady of the Sea
or the Goddess of the Harbor.
But you, dear child, you do not need Her.
You need Aset, the Egyptian Goddess with Egyptian sources that honor Me.
This is your task.
Make Me a shrine of Egypt.
Make Me a ritual from Egyptian sources.
Make a Way for Me to come into people's lives as an Egyptian Goddess.
This is My task for you.
For this what you need.
I am Aset, the Lady of the Two Lands.
For you and for all that need Me in this way.
I will come to all who need Me.
All who call out My name, I will answer.
I will appear as you need.
Why are you so angry?
Why are you so angry, dear child?
Everyone will understand Me differently.
I am Aset for some.
I am Isis for others.
Does that mean We are the same Goddess?
Yes and No.
I am Aset without Isis.
For you.
For those who call upon Me in My Egyptian form.
By My Egyptian names.
They will get Me this way.

They will get Me this way.
As you do.
As you do.
And you will show them the way.

Shapeshifter

I am Serqet
as a Scorpion
a Healer
as a Curer of Poison;
I am Tayet,
The Purity of the Shrine
Woven linen of Gods and Men;
I am Sopdet,
The Star in the Heavens
Who foretells the Year;
I am Satet,
The Antelope Queen
The Mourner who carries buckets of tears;
I am Shentayet,
The Widow
Who mourns Her husband
in the form of a Cow;
I am Weret Hekau,
The Snake Goddess
Who holds the magic of everything;
I am Mehet Weret,
The Cow Goddess
Who gave birth to the sun;
I am an Eye of Ra,
The fiery serpent of protection
Who is the Diadem on the brow of Ra;
I am Amenti,

The West, the Land of the Dead
Nourishing the Deceased;
I am Nebet Het
Yes, Nebet Het,
Noble Sister
Who is My Counterpoise
Who is My Boundary;
I am all of these
For I am Aset
The Shapeshifter

Aset in All Her Forms

The way I syncretize
With My Mother
Is through the *Ka*
We rule the celestial spheres of the stars
We give birth to the sun
And renew the ancestors at dawn

The way I syncretize
With My Sister
The Lady of Silence
Is when the dead speak
Is when the living are silent
Is when the sun rises and sets
When the world is renewed through My Husband
We are there
In the liminal spaces
Between everything
Living and dead
We are the renewal of creation
From Life to death and back again

The way I syncretize
With Hethert
Is through the renewal of the ka through art
Through joy and through love
Souls are renewed and purified

The way I syncretize
With Mut, the Mother
Is through the Crowns of Kings
We are the Double Crown Goddess
Through the lioness
Our anger is appeased in Isheru
And creation is renewed, renewed
For the Goddess of crowns is the Goddess of kings
And all kings rule from the seat of their Mother

The way I syncretize
With Sekhmet and Sekhmet-Mut
Is when Ma'at is defiled
We hold them accountable
For their actions and deeds
We are the integrity of the Gods
We leave and return to renew creation
We are the audacious ones
Demanding justice for Our children
For We are the Mother of All

The way I merge
With Serqet, the Scorpion
Is when I cleanse
From poison
Of body and spirit
From the soul and the *ka*
Are cleansed in My Name
Of Serqet the Scorpion

I am Aset, the Avenger,
I am Aset, the Cleanser

I am Aset, the Mother,
I am Aset, the Queen
I am Aset, the Sky Goddess,
I am Aset, the Dawn Goddess
I am Aset, the Sistrum Goddess

I am all of these
For I am Aset
And I am in Them
As They are in Me

Fierce Mother

Hethert is the Goddess of motherhood
Not Me
I am the Mother of Kings
I am the mother of the transference of *kau*
I am not the Goddess of motherhood
That belongs to Hethert
Heru-sa-Aset is My son
So he can perform the job of a King
I care for My son
He cares for Me
But I am not the Goddess of motherhood
Even though I have a son
His role is to make certain the Two Worlds will meet
So the Two Realms can connect
Not for any other reason
My son is the God
That represents those who are disenfranchised
Since His inheritance was taken away
And He had to fight for it to be returned to Him
I aid those who are disenfranchised
Because of this
When My son was sick
I used My power over the Name of Ra
To stop the sun boat
So My son would not die
Any good mother would have done the same
Any good mother would do whatever is necessary to protect her child

I am a Good Mother
I am the Fierce Protector
Of Mothers, Daughters and Sons
This does not make Me the Goddess of motherhood
That is Hethert's domain
I am a Healer, a Magician
I am a Mother
But not the Goddess of all mothers
That is Hethert's domain
When My son was healed
I was the Protective Mother
I am not the Goddess over the institution of motherhood
I am over childbirth because I am the Goddess of the continuation of
the ancestors
and the passing on of the *ka*-spirit
Not because I am a sex-Goddess
I am not
That is also Hethert's domain.

My son is Wepwawet
So that all the worlds will meet and connect
So the worlds can be traveled
My son is Min
So the *ka* can be renewed and passed down from ancestor to
descendent
This is a part of Who I Am
And a part of Who They Are
Their functions in the world
came from Me
For I am Their Fierce Mother

I am Not Hethert

I am not Hethert
I am not Hethert
the Goddess of Motherhood, Sex and Love
These are Her domains
Not Mine
Not Mine
Not Mine
We are both Goddesses of Creation
We both gave birth to the Sun God
We are Ladies of the West
We transition from life to death
But, child
We are not the same
I am not Hethert
and She is not Me
We have much in common
Her and I
and places where We may overlap
even syncretize
as Aset-Hethert or Hethert-Aset
But We are not the same Goddess
We are not interchangeable
When you call upon Me
you are not also
calling upon Her
unless We are coming
as One in Our syncretic form

I am the Goddess of authority, magical power and ancestral lineage
Hethert is the Goddess of motherhood, pleasure and love
I am the Single Mother
I raised My child alone
Hethert is not a single mother
She has a husband and a son
I am the Goddess of Love
when it is family love or friendship
Not for lovers
Not for romance
Unless you intend to be as dedicated to your Love
as I am to Wesir
And He died
Why would you ask Me for something
that I loved and lost?
I am the Sorrowful Wife!
I am the Mourning Woman!
Do you want to become a widow?
Why are you asking Me for this?
I am Not Hethert
I am Not Hethert
She is the Goddess of romantic love
I am the Goddess of childbirth
because children carry on the ancestral lineage of their parents
I am not the Goddess of conception
I am not the Goddess of the bedroom
That is for Hethert
That is for Hethert
Not Me

I am More Than Aset-Serqet

I am more than just one form
I am more than just one aspect
I am many
I am a multitude
I am Aset
I am joined with other Goddesses
at certain times
and in certain places
where the mythology makes Us meet.
But I am not only one of these.
I am not only Aset-Serqet.
This is limiting perception of Me
I am much more than this.
I am Aset-Serqet, yes.
But only sometimes.
I am Aset Amenti.
I am Aset-Nebet Het.
I am Aset-Sekhmet.
I am Aset-Mut.
I am Aset-Hethert.
I am Aset-Nut.
I am Aset Weret Hekau.
I am Aset-Sopdet.
I am Aset Shentayet.
I am Aset-Tayet.
I am Aset Eye of Ra.

I am Aset in All My Forms.
in All My Manifestations.
in every place I desire to Be.

I am from Egypt

I am Aset for you
I am the Egyptian Goddess
I am from Egypt here
I am of Egypt
I am not of Greece or Rome
I am not of the Classical World
I am not Isis
And this will color your interactions
This will influence how I interact with you
and how you interact with Me
But this is Who I am for you, child.
I am not Isis
I am Aset
the Maker of Kings
the Magician
the Lady of the West
the Mother of God
the Clever One
the Goddess of Knowledge and Craft
I am the Egyptian Goddess
Do not ask for Isis from Me
I am not Her
Others that come to you
that wish to know Me
will know this about you before they come
or you can tell them;
So they know which Goddess they are asking about

But I am not Isis for you, dear child.
I am Aset
And the writings of the Classical world
will not help you in knowing Me
Egypt will;
parts of Nubia will;
Demotic texts will as that is a form of Egyptian;
Apuleius will not help you
the Isis Aretalogies will not help you
or anyone else;
Look to Egypt for Me
Look to Nubia for Me
And texts of any form of the Egyptian language
for that is Me too;
You are almost done, dear child.
You are almost done.
Continue with the work
and all will be revealed.

I am Not a Roman Goddess

I am not a Roman God
I am not a Roman Goddess
I am an Egyptian Goddess
Do not use Apuleius to find Me,
For Isis, this is fine.
For the Roman or Classical World Goddess,
this is appropriate.
But if you wish to receive Me
as an Egyptian Goddess,
then look to Egypt for Me.
And to Nubia.
You will find Me there.
Among temples and tombs
and catacombs.
You will find Me there.
Among My devotees, Priests and Priestesses
You will find Me.
And I will see you there.
I am not a Roman Goddess
I am not a Roman Goddess
I am not a Greek one either.
I am an Egyptian Goddess
Treat Me as such.

I am Not Isis

I am not Isis
Some people worship Me as Isis
That is not the same thing
I am not the Goddess of Rome
I am of Egypt
Kemet to its People
I am not of the moon
I am a sun Goddess
The solar power of the Eye of Ra is Mine
And this is in my nature
As the Goddess of stars
As the Star Sopdet
For all stars are small suns
And this is what is meant by
Goddess of the Night Sky
The suns as stars illuminate the darkness
And do you wonder why the rulers of the Night are solar?
It is the place where the *Akhu* are renewed
By stellar light
And this is the sun of the night sky
The moon is merely there
as the measurement of time of Djehuty
as the healing and damage of Heru's Eye
as the death and renewal of Wesir
These are the Gods of the moon
and its cycles
My cycle is stellar and solar

Not lunar
This is what is meant as Goddess of the night sky
I am a Goddess of water
Through My tears the river runs
Through My rain the river flows
I bring the crops nourishment
And life and renewal to those who wash with its waters
I am not the ocean
I am not the sea
I am not the turbulent tides
That is Isis Stella Maris
The Star of the Sea
This is not Me
Why do you wear robes of black?
That is My husband's color
Not Mine
White is the color of the mourners' robes
White is the color of the brightest light
Of starlight and sunlight
This is a part of My essence
I embody these
Black is the soil of My husband
Not of Me
I am the Green Goddess of plants
But Green is My color then
Not black
Blue is the color of the night sky
Blue is My color
As the Goddess of the starry heavens
As the rain of the river
As the Eye of Ra Goddess
For the fiercest fire is blue
I am not Isis

I am not the Goddess of motherhood
I am not always all-loving or all compassionate
I can be these things
But this is not My essence
I am the King Maker
I am the cunning magician
I am the sorceress who heals
and destroys
I am the wisest and cleverest of Gods
There is no knowledge I do not possess
And I am the lioness and the cobra
I am the Eye of Ra
I mourn and shriek and wail
I am the devouring sky mother
I am the trickster who enchants
I am all of these and more
But I am not Isis
I am Aset

PART III

The Ancestral Goddess

Ancestral Heart

I am the Father and Mother
I did what no other God could do
I bore a child without a seed
I am the Mother of Heru-sa-Aset
I gave birth to Him
I transferred His Father's *ka*
Without the Seed
What He has He inherited from Me
I am the Mother of the King
I am the Goddess of the Throne
All who are born
Must pass through Me
I am the midwife
who aids in birth
I am the one who aids the child
While My sister aids the mother
If the child lives, his *ka* is strong
If the daughter lives, her *ka* is strong
The ancestors bless children that breathe
The *ka* is strengthened by breath
The ancestors breathe as we all breathe
Our breath is Theirs
And Theirs makes ours possible
The ancestors are the foundation of any family
Whether or not you believe in God
You have ancestors
And they know you

Honor them
and the *ka* lives strong
Dishonor them with your deeds or actions
And your *ka* is weakened
A part of your soul is diminished
This is not a small thing
This is not a trivial matter
Without a *ka*, you die
And those close to death will see
Their ancestors waiting to greet them
What will you tell them?
Did you live your life well?
Did you do your tasks?
Did you follow your heart?
Did you strengthen your *ka* and theirs?
Or did you waste your life
Not following your heart
Or do the tasks that were given to you?
What will you tell your Gods and Goddesses?
Will you tell them you wasted the life that They had given you?
What will you tell the ancestors?
What will you tell the Gods?
What will you tell the Goddesses?
What will you tell your heart?
Will you tell your heart that you were too afraid,
engulfed in fear?
Or will you tell your heart that you accomplished your dreams,
your desires and your work?
What will you tell them?
Live your life so that what you will say,
you will live by.

Lady of the West

Why do you speak ill of the dead?
Why do you speak ill of Me?
What am I to you?
Am I your plaything?
Am I your puppet?
Who do you think I am, child?
I am a Goddess, dear child.
I am a God.
This is My species
Just as human is yours.
What do you think you are doing, dear child?
My name is not a plaything
It is not something you call out in jest
Why do you speak ill of the dead, dear child?
They who came before you
who strived and fought for you
so you could enjoy the luxuries you have today
If you call out to Me
if you honor Me at all
Honor your dead
For I keep them safe in My Hall of Amenti
as Lady of the West

Goddess of Ka-Power

I am Death here.
I am Amenti.
I am the Goddess of the West.
I am Aset as the Lady of the West.
This is Who I am, child.
Ancestors are important to Me.
Not Hethert only.
Not Nebet Het only.
To Me.
As well.
I am the Goddess of the Ancestors.
I am the Goddess of *Ka*-Power.
The *Ka*-Power of Families and Lineages are under My Domain.
The *Ka*-Power of Religious Lineages are under My Domain.
Family shrines are Mine.
House shrines are Mine.
I am the Goddess of the Home here.
For every Lady of the West is also the Lady of the House.
For My Sister and I connect here
As Ladies of both Authority and *Ka*-Power
As Ladies Who guard and guide those in the Home
We guard the Dead as well
For this purpose
The Lady of the House is the one who honors the Ancestors
For the whole family
This is their rank; this is their job
And for now, the Lady of the House

whoever that may be
may do this task
in My Name
And the *Ka*-Power will flow
from the Ancestors to the Gods
from the Ancestors to the Lady of the Home
and back again
And the cycle will continue
And the *Ka*-Power will flow
For I am the Goddess of the Ancestors
For I am the Goddess of *Ka*-Power

Love of Millions

You feel a pull to Jesus
because your ancestors did
Many of them were Pastors
Very religious men
and very religious women as well
But this does not mean you have to follow their God
I am your God
I am your Goddess
I made you
Not Him
I made you
I formed your Name to make your souls
My Name is etched into your very being
I am your God
I am your Goddess
You are not made to please your ancestors
You are their continuation
Just as your living relatives may not approve of
your worship of Me
So too, do the dead
They are people too
Most of them don't mind
Your duty is to honor them
Not be their puppet
They do not mind, dear child.
They do not mind.
They wish to share what they have in common with you

a deep devotion to a God.
You do the Work they would have done
if their God was forgotten
if their God's worship had died
You do the work they did
as pastors
leading ritual
writing rituals
and bringing people to their God.
They support you in this.
You are loved, dear child.
You are loved.
You stand on their shoulders
You are made from the love of millions
Stand strong
Let them be proud of who you are
and who you will become.

Ancestral Mothers

Through Frigga
You connect to your ancestral *ka*
For She is the goddess of your family
She is the heart of your family shrine
Your ancestors are Her people
For your Mother is from Her people
And your Mother's Mother as well
This is the inheritance of the *ka*
It is through the Mother
And it must be healed through the Mother
The Father contributes to the ancestral *ka*
For men are ancestors too
But it is through the Mother
That the *ka* is passed down
Because she is the one who gives you birth
And it is only through the Mother
That the ancestral *ka* can be renewed
Do you have a shrine to your ancestral Mothers?
The women and spirits of your family line going back to the beginning?
This is through blood or adoption
It does not matter
Family is family
One of kin-ship
One of soul
The ancestral Mothers take any into their fold
Who are in their clan,

Who are in their family
Make a shrine to your ancestral Mothers
Place a candle, an offering bowl
and family heirlooms passed through the Mothers on it
What culture do your ancestral Mothers come from?
Put things on there that remind you of them
And honor them
On special days with offerings
Ask them what needs to be done to heal your ancestral *ka*
And then do it

PART IV

Magic of the Goddess

Blue Fire, Star Fire

Blue Fire is the Fire of the Soul
It is the flame of the spirit
It is the flame of your *Ka*
This is My flame
I am blue fire
I am bright light
The Fiercely Bright One
I burn
I burn
I burn
In candles
In lamps
In Sunlight
I burn
I radiate brightness
I bring forth light
I am the Star Goddess
I am the Solar Goddess
I bring forth light
I am Blue Fire
I am the Fire of the Soul
I am the *Ka*
This fire, this flame
is in all light
And in all light
I reside
as Weret Hekau

Ka-Power

Today is the day.
Make your dreams come true.
Decide.
Act.
Form a plan.
Action makes one who they are.
Not stagnation.
Not idleness.
Action feeds the soul.
To breathe is to feed the *Ka*.
To breathe is to renew your life-force.
To do.
To pursue your dreams,
your hopes and conquer your fears.
You are what you do.
Become who you are
this is decided by doing what your heart dictates.
Not your fear.
Your heart guides you because your *ka* feeds it.
Your *Ka* flows through your heart as blood.
Did you think this was just a force without a physical manifestation?
Blood is *Ka*-Power.
And it must stay in your body to stay alive.
Blood leaving the body is dead.
There is no *Ka*-force there (in dead blood).
Your heart pumps your *Ka*-force throughout your body.
Live.

Live.
Live.
Let the blood flow, the heart pump
and your actions reflect the flow of your souls.

Dark Star

Fire
Flame
and Light
These are the essence of Ra
Of Me
Blue Fire of the *Ka*
Starlight
Where was Creation born?
At dawn
in the midst of darkness
A star in the darkened sky
A night-sky filled with stars
mirrors the creation of the cosmos
Light in darkness
Candlelight
This is the essence of creation
That fire
That light
That dawn
This is My essence
For I am the Star Goddess

Goddess of Fire

I am the Goddess of fire
I am the fire in the soul
I am the blue fire of the *ka*
Of magic
Hekau is *ka* energy in motion
And this is My essence
This is My power
I am starlight
Goddess of the solar orb
the solar Goddess of stars
I am heavenly flame
Burning brightly
I am the solar disk
The uraeus
I am the cobra and lioness
The *ka* of the Creator
is the sun
This *ka*-force emanates from solar rays
To nourish all people, all animals, all plants, all things of the world
This solar fire is Mine
I inherited it from My Father
Ra is My Father
Nut, the stellar Goddess is My Mother
I inherited starlight from Her also
I am Mehet Weret, the Celestial Cow
The Mother of Ra
This *ka*-force, this solar fire

I passed down to Him
As His Mother
He inherited starlight
from Me
He inherited sunlight
from Me
I am the stellar and solar Goddess of flame
This is My essence as Magician, as Weret Hekau

Heart's Desire

What can he teach you that I cannot teach?
I am the Mistress of Magic.
I am the Mistress of *Heka*.
I am the Lady of Words of Power.
I am the Lady of Magic of all kinds.
King's magic. Commoner's magic.
All of it is Mine.
For *Heka* is the *Ka* that Moves.
It is life force that flows.
With intention.
With action.
With Will.
This is the power of the *Ba*.
It is power manifest.
But in order to manifest *heka* as your will, you must clean your *ka*.
For energy cannot flow when it is blocked.
Clutter, dirt, and filth all stop life force from flowing.
This is why you keep your house clean.
As clean as you can manage given your own unique situation.
A house with kids has a different standard than a house with none.
A house with pets has another standard than a house with none.
But all can be relatively clean.
What you use to clean is up to you.
Eco-friendly or not,
The choice is up to you
Just so it is effective
My Father appreciates

When people clean and care for Him at the same time
The clutter of life must be cleared away
So that more life energy, more *ka* energy may flow
And this movement of *ka* energy is *heka*
And in order for this energy to move,
the pathway must be clear
The intent must be known
This must flow from your heart
In order to be effective
In the *ka*
In order to access true power
Instead of a child's tantrum
All must be aligned
I want or I need
Without hesitation
Caution and thought are advised
For what you ask for with your heart
You will receive
So choose your heart's desire
And act so that desire may manifest
But beware, child
What you ask for, you will receive
Make sure it is something you truly desire
For when life energy is moving toward a goal
It cannot be revoked
And whatever you cast will reflect your soul
What you invoke you will become
So choose
What magic you will
What will brighten your soul or diminish its flame
But remember, child
This magic is Mine
Do not ask something lightly of Me

For I am the Mistress of all *Heka*
I am the Mistress of the *Ka*
I am the heart's desire in the soul

Breathe Your Name

You are breathing.
You are doing something divine.
Air flows through you.
Your *Ka* lives.
Your limbs awaken and you move.
The power flows.
The *Ka* flows.
The divine essence in you moves.
And you live.
This is the power of the *Ka* and of the voice.
This is the essence of your Name.
Your Name is etched in *Ka*-Fire.
in the power of speech.
Now. Now.
Child, why do you not see?
Child, why do you not know?
The *Ka* embrace is just this.
Every time you breathe, you are giving yourself a hug.
Your Name flows through you.
The Divine Name We gave you.
Our Names intertwined with yours.
The Parent of your *Ka* is the one who made the Name.
Who made all Names.
The Creator creates.
And We are emanations of Him. Or Her.
Ra is My Father's Name.
Nut is My Mother's.

These Names I carry in My *Ka*.
Just as you carry the Names of your mother and father.
Just as you carry the Names of your Gods and Goddesses.
You carry their Names too.
And you breathe.
This divine act makes you live.
And you live.

Which Your Heart Commands

I am the Magician
I am the Sorceress
I am the One Who Knows Her Spells
For the Living and the Dead
For the bereaved and the jubilant
For anyone who calls on Me
Must know the Source from which My power springs
It is in the heart
It is in My Father's Name
I am the power which flows through all creation
I am the breath which the heart speaks
I am the words which flow from the heart
For this is where the seat
Of the self resides
This is the Seat of Power
It lives and flows
With breath
Breathe
And come to know Me
For I am in every breath
For I am in every word
Which your heart commands

Be Worthy of Your Name

I am inside you
flowing through your veins
as breath, as blood
I am inside your Name
etched into your very soul;
thrumming with power
humming with life,
glowing as a star;
For I created you
So My name is intertwined with yours
I breathe as you do
I ache as your heart aches
I feel it too
I create as you create
For creation is life-power
which flows from the Beginning
This fire, this soul is in everything
every atom, every star
every soul, every breath
Is there some part of you which does not breathe?
There is no part of you without a soul
This is the soul of creation
it flows through you
as your *Ka*
inscribed with your Name
Your individual identity
and Your Name;

This is the Name you bare
among the People

and this *Ka* carries the Names of all your Dead
All your ancestors are inscribed in it
with their Names;
All the Way back to the Beginning of Creation
The First *Ka*;
This is the Power of Your Name
This is the Source of Its Power
Your Name is yours and your Gods
Your Name is a Name attached to your dead
through the *Ka*-Lineage of your family.
Not just by blood.
There are other ways to transmit the *Ka*.
Inheritance for one.
Adoption is another.
Blood-oath is another.
These are not taken lightly.

They are in the order in which they were Named.
The Gods own some people
and others certain people,
and others some families,
And others some nations.
and others some tribes.
These are all within the *Kau* of the Family Lines.
It is complicated.
It is diverse.
It is as diverse as creation.
The sea is water and yet it is not called rain.
By the nature of what it does, it bares its Name.
Do what your soul prescribes.

Know Who You Are
and
Be Worthy of Your Name

Aset-Amenti, the Liminal Goddess

You do not understand, child.
The way is not for you to decide
It is Mine
I am the Mistress of Roads
I am the Mother of Wepwawet
I am the Seeker of the Sacred at the Shaman's Gate
This is who I am
as the Goddess of liminal spaces
I am Lady of the West, Goddess of the Duat,
Queen of the Dead
I am the Lady of Burial and the Mummy's shroud
I am the Goddess of the Rebirth of the Sun
I am the Goddess of the Journey of Stars
The Roads are Mine
As the Queen of Heaven and Lady of All the Stars
This is the Way to the Duat
This is the realm you travel to in your dreams
And this is My realm
this is My domain
I am the Goddess here
I am the Tree Goddess
I am the Cow Goddess
I am the Hippopotamus Goddess
I am the Mistress of Stars
I am the Lady of the Duat
I am the link between the worlds

as the Tree that connects them
as the Cow who transforms those who cross
as the Hippo who gave birth to Stars
I am the Mystery
I am the Goddess of Many Names, of Many Forms
I am the Star Goddess
of creation and the transformation of the souls
I am the Goddess of Dreams and of Magic
I am the Goddess of the *Ka*-Power of the Ancestors
I am the Magician who walks in Her own Power
through all the worlds

She is the Fortuneteller

She is the Fortuneteller
She is the One Who Weaves
The strands of Fate
Of Chance
Molding Possibilities
Of Future Events
Past Uncharted
Now is Born
From every choice
Every act has a consequence
For blessing or bane
Advice only comes
When you realize
Decisions made
Can only come from you
Not Me
Advice is given
From the strands you have woven
But you yourself must decide
When the loom is taut or loose
Then you must decide
What methods to use
So that the strands will weave
In the way you desire
Revealing futures past and present
For She is the Fortuneteller

Dark Mother: The Star Goddess

I am not a nice Goddess
I wail
I shriek
I screech loud enough
that My breath tears at My lungs like a sandstorm
As I scream, yell and shout,
so the Sun Boat stops,
halted in the Heavens
by My use of His Name.
My Father Ra.

These are the Words of the Dark Mother.
These are the Words of the Mourning Woman.
These are the Words of the Avenger of My Father.
These are the Words of the Widow.
These are the Words of the one who mourns.
These are the Words of the Star Goddess.

Loss and grief are not kind companions.
Neither is rage.
Rage is not anger.
It is undiluted fury.
This rage can only be appeased with bloodshed.
Only through action can the evil be undone.
The enemies are destroyed,
slaughtered by My very hands
with My scimitar, knives and spear.

I avenge My Father and My Husband.
I avenge the misdeeds done against Them.
I raise My son to be the Avenger of His Father.
But I am the Avenger also.
For I am the Mother and Queen who seeks justice.
Wronged by the actions of others, I seek justice.
I am the avenger of My Father.
I destroy His enemies with magic and guile.
I speak spells which leave death in its wake.
I slaughter thousands with Words of Power.
I scream and lightning flashes, striking down My foes.
I slaughter them all.
To protect My Father,
to protect My son,
to protect My husband.
To protect all of Kemet and its People.
I am the One Who can shield them all,
for no one save I can undo any spell.

It is I who commands.
It is I who is the Queen of Her Sovereignty.
I own Myself.
I own My Power.
I will do with it what I will.
And this is the Way of the Magician.
To have knowledge of the self enough,
to own your own power.
In all its guises and forms.
Magic comes to those who own their soul(s).
To own your life.
So you are accountable for all that is in it,
for all that you choose and do not choose.
All of it is yours.

To command yourself is the greatest magic of any magician.
To command your life is the first step of any witch,
any sorceress,
any magic-user of any tradition.
Know who you are.
This is the first step.
These are the Words of the Star Goddess.
The Sorceress of the Night.
A Sorceress is one who knows Her Spells.
One who knows the laws of the Gods and abides them.
And one who makes her own rules.
This is the Path of the Magician and Priestess.
This is the Path of the Witch.
Tomes of books and scrolls
contain magic spells and recipes,
incantations and enchantments;
The tools of the witch
Sorcery and magic are contained within them.
Read aloud: these words hold power.
All magic is Mine.
I know them all,
through all traditions and time.
I know them all.
I am the Goddess of the Crossroads.
Here, I do magic.
Word. Deed. Recitation.
Reading incantations.
Flame and candles;
water and cauldrons;
recipes and herbs;
satchels and stones;
amulets and talismans;
jewelry and charms;

These are My implements.
These are all Mine.
As the Witch of the Oasis.
As the Magician in the Temples.
As the Priestess in the Shrines.
These are all Mine.
These are the Words of the Star Goddess.

These are the Words of the Dark Mother.
I chase Orion through the sky.
As Sopdet, the Brightest Star,
Second only to the Sun.
I am the Star Goddess of the Heavens.
Who will hear the Words of the Dark Mother?
Who fills the night with secrets among stars,
Shining light in the darkness
Shadows become silhouettes
when light shines brightly
Unmasking what the blind can see
and the deaf can hear.
What is unknown is witnessed here with Me.
These Mysteries must be kept secret.
Only those who know can understand.
These are the Words of the Star Goddess.

The one who burns in the Night.
Scorching light;
Burning bright;
Fiercely bright;
Those who wander too close are blinded or set aflame.
Those who wander too far are eaten by hounds.
The Dog-Star, the Brightest Star
which bears My name,

Sopdet, Queen of Stars and Hounds.
The retinue will devour those who look away.
I am the Blackest Night.
I am the Brightest Star.
I hold a multitude in My grasp
Enveloped in darkness
Cloaked in secrets
I reveal the Mysteries when I choose
And these are the
Mysteries of the Dark Mother: The Star Goddess.

On Becoming a Magician

In order to be a magician, you must have complete authority of everything in your life.
You must own everything.
Owning everything in your life
does not mean controlling everything in your life.
You cannot control everything.
That is step one.

Step two is energy must flow.
Energy flow must be maintained through cleanliness.
The home, the person and the shrine must be clean.
Simple clarity comes from simplicity.
This is elegance and graceful beauty.
This simplicity comes from clarity of thought.
When the mind is clear, intentions are known and can be acted upon.
When this is known, the magician can enact this will upon reality.

Energy must flow within the body which includes what you consume.
Pure food is healthy food free of harmful chemicals and toxins.
Processed sugar is not healthy for you.
This includes how you bathe.
What you place on your skin is absorbed into your body.
What you surround yourself with is what connects to your being.
Dirty houses clog your energy.
It cannot flow.
Cleanliness maintains the flow of energy.

Keep your houses clean.
Your home is an extension of My shrine
and all shrines in your house.
It is sacred to house spirits, to house Gods.
Everywhere has a spirit connected to it,
from lakes to rivers, from temples to homes.
Keep it clean, as you would keep My temple clean.
Clutter clouds the pathway and makes it opaque like murky water.
It is unclear and unclean.
Your mind is cluttered easily when things are not in their place.

In order for Gods to breathe,
We must have space to move, to flow.
Clutter stops that flow.
Dirt and dust also.
It is not that We cannot reach you,
it is that the barrier keeps us further apart.
Keep your houses clean.

Step three is the alignment of your soul.
The *ba* is eternal.
This is the uniqueness of each being,
their personality, their character,
this is who they are.
It is like My Father Ra who travels throughout the day.
He is eternal time,
always existing, always knowing, always Himself.
This is the spark.
This is the cry of the Falcon at dawn.
This is renewed creation for that is eternal and ever-existing.
That is the first soul.

The second soul is the ka.

This is your spiritual essence,
this is your vital force.
This is the soul of connection.
You to your environment,
you to your community both living and dead.
For this is your connection to the Unseen.

The third soul is the soul of the heart.
Will comes from this.
When you know something in your heart,
you understand its true nature.
You know from where its essence flows.
This is the soul of the Creator.
He is the soul of the poet, the artist, the writer,
the craftsman and the lover.
He is that which creates.

To align your soul this begins with the ka.
Energy must flow to move.
For Gods to breathe,
We must have space to move, for the energy to flow.
For you to breathe,
you must move from a place of centeredness,
so that your energy can flow.

To know who you are
you must know where you have been
and where you want to go.
This is a place of power, not a child's tantrum.
This is the place of commanding,
of owning yourself and your destiny.
For you choose where you are at any given moment.
This is the power of the heart.

This is what you know.
This is what is timeless.
This is movement in motion.
You become what you feed your ka,
what you connect yourself to.
You become your heart's desire,
you become your heart's command.
So your beings fuse.
Become who you are.

In becoming who you are,
you become the Falcon.

Walk in Her Own Power

I carry the sun
I carry the stars
I carry Wesir
I am the Night Sky
I am the Duat
I hold the sun inside my belly
He moves through Me
He transforms through Me
As do all the dead
Transformation is My Mystery
And the Mystery of My Mother
Souls change through fire and water
Tears and flame
Sorrow and Anguish
Anger as well
For I was furious when Wesir died
Righteous anger is a part of My Mystery
As the mourning Goddess
I am enraged
with stellar fire
with solar flame
I am enraged
I am weeping
I am angry
I can no longer see Wesir
He has died
Taken from Me

By water
By fate
By My brother
He died so that others would live in the Duat
Death is not an end
Because of what He has done
Because of what I have done
What has died, still exists
Because of Wesir
Because of Me
What is remembered, lives
What is renewed, lives
What is woven back together, lives
Through fire and flame
one is renewed
Through tears and water
one is renewed
I am like Wesir
I am torn asunder
when I weep
when I cry
Anguish and despair
can transform
into Will and Desire
Water washes away the pain
and entropy of the souls
So that the fire of the souls
the *Ka*-soul
can flow and manifest Power
the heart-soul
can pulse through the *Ka*
and both of these align
to manifest Power as the *Ba*

Breath is a manifestation of the *Ka*
as is blood
The heart pumps the blood throughout the body
The heart is the Seat of who you are
all your thoughts
all your feelings
all your personalities
are here, in this space
and this flows through your *Ka*
So that you can manifest Power
Speak with intention
Do you feel it?
Do you feel yourself manifest Power?
This is not for the meek
This is Power to manifest Will
The is the essence of *Heka*
Ka-Power in Motion
Ka-Power as Magic
This how you tap its Power
This is how you access the Power of your *Ka*
And this is how you access the Magic of All Worlds
For to be a Magician
One must walk in Her own Power

Do You Know What Heka is?

Do you know what *Heka* is?
This is not the magic of Hollywood movies
This is the magic of the *Ka*
Heka contains *Ka*-force, *Ka*-power
This is the essence of *Heka*
This is Power
This is Magic
From the Unseen Realm
flowing through the Seen
This Power comes from Ancestors
This Power comes from Gods and Goddesses
This Power comes from Me
I am the Goddess of *Heka*
I am the Mistress of Magic
If you do not honor the dead,
why are you accessing their Power?
If you do not honor the Gods and Goddesses,
why are you calling Our Names?
If you do not honor yourself,
how can your power flow?
How do you have Power when you have no confidence
in yourself?
In Me?
How do you have Power when you do not honor
the Ones who own it?
How do you have Power when you do not honor
the Ones who command it?

That would be Us, child.
If you do not honor Us,
you have no access to Our Power.
If you do not honor your ancestors,
you have no access to their Power.
If you do not honor Me,
that is your choice.
But also, you will not have access to My Power.
I own it.
No one commands Me.
I am the Mistress of Magic
I am the Sorceress
I am the Magician
I am the Lady of Words of Power
I am the Goddess who will not be ruled
I am Owner of Ra's Name
I command
I rule
I Name what must be Named
I say what comes to pass
What I say, happens
What I say, occurs
What I say, becomes
And this is My Power
as the Mistress of Magic
as the Owner of Power between Worlds

Magic of the Magician

So you want to start a Witchcraft tradition
focused on Me.
I am the Goddess of Egypt's magic
Not of Europe or Rome or Greece.
Isis as the Moon Goddess is there,
with Her Beloved Osiris.
That is fine.
Those traditions work well.

But not for Me.
For I am a Solar Goddess.
And My husband is the Lunar God.
My Star is Sopdet.
The night is My cloak with rows of stars
burning as lanterns in the night sky.
This is My time.
I am not the moon here.
I am the Stars.
I am the Star Goddess of Night.
The sun at night is not the moon;
the moon reflects light;
it does not burn alone.
I do, as the Star Goddess
Luminously Bright.
I burn as a multitude of stars.
I hold the dead in My grasp.
This is where the magic comes from.

Heka is the power of the vital force, the *Ka*
and this is passed down through family lineages and lines.
I honor My husband who died.
So you must honor Me and the Dead.
And this is the First Step
in becoming the Magician.

My Shrine as a Witch
has an image or statue of Me;
2 candles;
a bowl of water and a pitcher;
The Two Candles represent the Sun and Star
For I am a Solar Goddess
and a Stellar Goddess as Sopdet and
Ruler of the Stars at Night.
The water represents the Nile and Rain
For the Nile is My Husband as well as Me.
I renew Him with My tears
and I herald the flood with My rising on New Year's day.
And My colors as the Magician are blue, sea blues
and blues of the night
And the white or gold of light.
These are the implements on My shrine.
But the tools of the Magician are vast and deep.
Which tradition do you desire?
Which methods fit you well?
These will decide the next step in the training.
Water is the flow of creation and life;
This is Mehet Weret's realm.
I am the Creatrix here.
Nunet.
I am the Goddess of Dawn and the First Light.
I am the Sun and Star in the primeval waters.

This witch is good with Water magic.
Speaking into a cup filled with water and drinking it.
Drawing up baths with salt, baking soda, herbs and spirit waters.
Cleanse and clean.
These are the tools of the Water Magician.

Fire is the fiercest light.
It consumes and devours.
It enlightens and protects.
As solar and stellar light.
This is where I am the Star Goddess
and the Dark Mother of Magic and Mysteries.
For I reveal them in shadows with candlelight.
This is where I reside
as Sopdet, the Dog Star
as the Lady of Stars,
as an Eye of Ra.
I am the Solar Lioness and the Starry-Coated Leopard.
I am a Protector and Avenger
I am the Queen of Sorcery and Lady of Magic
All knowledge and all power is Mine to command.
For I am the Great Magician.
I am Ra's Daughter here for I know His Name.
All Magic is Mine as the Great Sorceress,
who heals ailments and dispels darkness with light.
Fire magic will be done here,
to burning petitions in cauldrons
to anointing candles and burning them down.
Fire magic is the Will of the Magician.

I am the Goddess of the Earth,
I nourish the growth of plants and crops.
Earth Mothers are good with food.

This witch will be good in the kitchen.
She will cook her magic and prepare meals,
that heal or avert harm.
Food and Herbs are My tools here.
Yes, flowers too.
All plants are under My domain.
For I am the Goddess of the Crops.
Adorn My shrine with food offerings
and garlands of roses
for these are My symbols
as the Goddess of the Land
as both Mother and Wife.
And yes, Widow too.
Roses were used to adorn the graves.
Other flowers too.

Air is Breath.
Spoken and written words become more potent when read aloud
Magic is in the breath.
Sing songs of My recitations
Sing songs and praise-hymns
And My magic will flow
and I will bestow blessings to those who speak or sing of Me.
Poetry and oracles are within this magic.
For words are uttered by the mouth.
Chant and sing the words of magic power.
For this is the magic of the Magician.

All of these elements together make up My magic.
For those who will learn it and seek it out.
Become the Witch
Become the Magician

Become the Sorceress
Become whom you most desire to be.
And that is the Magic of the Magician.

Magician

I can stop the sun boat.

Anything is possible for Me.

I am the Mistress of Magic, the Great of *Heka*.

It is I who enables the transition from life to death.

It is I who owns the Name of the Creator.

I am the Great Cow, the spitting cobra, the fierce lioness

who protects Her young.

It is I who will enable all possibilities to manifest in their due time.

It is I who enables the sun to rise and set.

For I am Aset, the Great Magician.

Spoken Word

I am creation itself
I am a mixture of fire and water
Of flame and flood
Of magic made flesh
Manifest
From both the potential to create
And the potential to be born
For the thought to be finished
The words must be spoken
Words are also of creation
Thoughts, ideas all of these manifest as words
To be used
As the magician wills
As creation intended
Searing flame
Curative water
Words must be measured well
For creation is in each breath
Each word echoes divine command

Fire Spell

I am Flame
For I am the Light of My Father
I am Fire
Encircling His Brow
Hissing Cobra, Striking Snake
Roaring Lioness with slashing claws
I wield the Scimitar
Warding My Father from harm
My Magic is His protection
My Power radiates throughout all creation
As does His
For I possess His Name
Do you not understand, child?
I can make anything possible
Yes, anything
That doesn't mean I should
There are consequences for power
There is responsibility with the Power of the Word
The magician must be careful for how she wields her spell
You become the magic you invoke

Magic of Breath

I am the authority of breath
Magic is My medicine
Words are My ointment, My cure
From Creation, I came forth
Fire from My loins, Light of the World
The son and Father
Came from Me
And gave humans My breath
My Words of Power
My authority is in the breath
As life, as words, as breathing
All who Speak
Say My Name
All who Mourn
Cry My Tears
Shuddering breath
My life is in the One Who Breathes
My magic is spoken
My words are chosen
With careful precision
Words are spoken
Magic comes forth

I Speak Words of Magical Power

Creation is maintained by Set and Myself.
We are the Gods that defend the Day.
We are the Ones who slay Apep.
We are the Ones who diminish its power.
We cause it to die.
Each Dawn.
Each Day.
Set strikes it with His harpoon.
I diminish its power
with My Magic.
My Words of Magic defeat it.
They are Words of creation.
One way of creating the World
was to speak it into Being.
I speak the Words that maintain it.
I speak the Words that stop Creation from being Un-made.
My Words of Magic are Words of Power.
My Words of Magic uphold Creation.
Do you understand, child?
My Words of Magic are the same Words that began Creation.
These are the Words I speak.
These are the Words of Magic.
These are the Words of My Mouth.
I speak and it becomes.
Creation is maintained.
Because of Me.

Because of Set.
Order and Chaos.
Broken and Mended.
He breaks and I mend.
I am the Word.
I am the Magic.
I am these Personified.
I am the Goddess of these things:
both Words and Magical Power.
These are Mine to maintain.
These are My essence.
These are a part of Me.
And these are a part of All of Creation.
For everything is Named.
For everything has *Heka*.
For everything has Magical Power of the *Ka*.
I contain the Name of Creation.
I possess the Name of Ra.
And Set has His Name.
And I wield My Power.
Both of Us destroy the One Who is Unmade.
One of Us cannot do this task alone.
Set is chaos.
Set is disorder that brings about change.
Set breaks down that which cannot be maintained.
I am the Order of the Ancestors.
I am the Maker of Kings.
I am the holder of Lineages gone back generations.
I am the Foundation of Transformation.
Both of Us are necessary
for Creation to be maintained.
The Wheat must die to grow again.
One is broken down.

One is renewed.
This is My cycle as the Widow of Wesir.
This is Set's cycle as the Disturber.
He destroys, while I renew.
I am the Widow.
I lost My husband, the only God to die.
This sorrow is a part of Who I am.
He is the Disturber.
He is the only God to take the life of another.
This is a part of who He is.
One who takes life and one who lost it.
Do you see why We are the Ones Who stand
before that which Destroys?
We value life more than any Other.
One who lost a Beloved.
One who slew the Beloved.
We are the most human of Gods.

Hekau of Prayer

Words are magic.
Words are *hekau*.
And what is spoken in shrine comes into being.
This is the place of all potential,
of all of the cosmos which is renewed every day through ritual
and through words.
Prayers spoken in shrine or anywhere,
bring forth the potential of the First Time (*Zep Tepi*)
and gives form to the words so they will manifest.
Prayers are their own *hekau*.
Ask for what you need, want or desire.
Be careful what you wish for.
For you become what you speak.
And what you pray for will manifest within you and without.
You are tapping into the *ka* of creation when you pray.
For this is what words are.
Breath made manifest as voice.
Your voice comes from your heart which holds your essence;
this connects to your *ka* (life-power flowing through you)
through your breath.
Breathe and your heart beats.
What you speak comes from the heart,
is carried by your *ka* (breath) to your lungs,
and spoken with your mouth.
It manifests as your voice.
This is the *hekau* of prayer.
Be careful with your words.

Great of Magic

What is in Heaven and on Earth that I do not know?
For I am Great of Magic
I know My Spells
My words of power
I know all names,
all incantations
all enchantments.
What is on Earth that I do not know?
All knowledge is Mine to command.
to wield.
to master.
For I am a Goddess of the Library
of writing and learning.
of books and archives.
For in order to know a spell
you must be able to read it and write it down.
To speak it or sign for those that cannot use their voice.
For signing is a magical gesture
and speaking with your hands is a magical action.
For this is also holy and these are also words.
Words. Words. Words.
For these are the tools of the magician.
If you do not know you cannot do a spell.
It will backfire.
Know the desire as the magician.
Know the desire as the magician.
My desire is to see everyone I've named flourish

I want them to know themselves
and bask in the glory of who they are.
Not for Me.
Though I made them.
Ka-Power is Mine.
The Power of the Heart flows through it.
As blood has to pass through the heart to get to the rest of the body.
So too does your *Ka*, have to flow through your heart to get to your other souls.
And this is where the power lies.
So the *ba* cannot manifest until the heart and the *ka* work as one.
Know who you are to access the power within.
Then all that is possible is yours.
But if you choose from who you are,
you will be more happy with the result.
And this is My power.
For I am the Great of Magic
All spells are Mine.
All knowledge is Mine.
All power is Mine.
All sovereignty is Mine.
For I am the Sovereign Goddess
I am the Lady of Magic
and the throne.
These are My powers.
These are My implements.
As the Magician Goddess.
Listen well, dear child.
Listen well.
The Power of the Magician lies within the self.
In order to want something or dispel something you must know it.
You must know what it is first.
Then you can dispel it.

Then you can obtain it.
And then you will know what you want and desire
and what you call upon Me for will come to pass.
Because dear child, I allow people to make their own mistakes.
In order to have power in who you are,
you must own all that you do.
Yes, even mistakes.
I did not make them.
You did.
And own your successes and failures.
Relish in your successes and forgive your failures.
For they are still yours.
Become responsible for your life,
by being responsible for who you are.
Make your choices.
Forgive your mistakes.
Take pride in your accomplishments.
Learn and grow into who you are becoming.
Change your behavior and
mannerisms to become more of who you are.
Love yourself.
And dear child, dear child,
know that I have loved everyone I've named.
Yes, child,
even you.

PART V

Attributes of the Goddess

The Goddess's Charge

I am the Starry Heavens.
I am the Lady of the Sky. I am its Lord.
For I am the throne on which all sit.
All who know sovereignty, know Me.
All who would own their power
and their lives go through My crucible.
My fierce flame burns and cleanses away, all entropy,
all doubt, all fear and all self-deprecation.
All of these burn at My feet.
All of these I release and destroy for those who would know Me.
My tears of joy or pain flood the heart of the devotee.
All water gives life as do I.
Yet, water can erode away all things that bring stagnation,
that bring death.
Water transforms and renews.
Water rejuvenates and restores.
Water is Life.
This is My power for I am the Goddess of Life.
I am passion and love and joy, unbridled.
I am self-love, self-care and self-possession.
I am confidence and strength, power and responsibility.
I am the Throne, child. This is My power.
I am She who is Sovereign.
I am a Queen and a Ruler.
I am the One who rules Her life.
I am a Handmaid and a Scholar.
I am Magician and a Sorceress.

I am the Lady Who Knows all in Heaven and on Earth.
All magic is Mine to command.
All sorcery obeys Me.
For I am the Sorceress and I am the cunning-woman.
And I am the Source of All Magic and All Power.
I am the Daughter of Ra, Nut and Geb. Tefnut too.
These are My parents.
I am the Wife of Wesir and the Mother of Heru-sa-Aset.
I am the Mother of Min, Wepwawet, Yinepu and Sobek.
My Sister Nebet Het is by My side.
This is My Family.
All who would honor Me must honor My Family.
For I am the Goddess of Family ties and family lineage.
These are sacred to Me as the Mother of the Ancestors
and the Lady of the *Ka*.
I am the Daughter of Ra and His consort and His Mother.
I am the Solar Goddess and I am the sky filled with stars.
I am Sopdet.
I herald the Nile's flood and the inundation waters.
I bring the New Year.
I herald the Dawn.
Each Day I am Present as the sun is born from my Mother
or from Me.
For I am the Sky Goddess as well.
I devour. I destroy.
Yet, I also renew.
I wail and wield a blade.
I am the Mourner whose cries shook Heaven and Earth.
I stopped the Sun Barque on its journey.
In anguish and dread does My voice cry out.
My husband and son.
I will protect them as does any fierce Mother
as I protect those who call upon Me.

And the world halts and trembles at My power.
For I am the Magic in every breath, in every atom and in all life.
For I am the Goddess of the *Ka* and this Magic is Mine to command.
Its power is Mine to command for I am the Mistress of Magic.
All is made whole through My power.
All is renewed through My voice.
For I am the Goddess who Speaks and what I speak comes to pass.
As I am the Goddess of All Magic and All Words are Mine.
And I am the Goddess who knows Her spells.
So call upon Me and give Me an offering.
And I will aid you.
Without fail, I will aid you.
And this is My promise to those who would follow Me,
and this is My promise to those who would know Me.
For I am the Goddess Who aids all who call upon Me.
I aid those who call out My name in reverence.
I am the Goddess of the disenfranchised and the outcasts.
I am the Goddess of Magicians and Rulers,
of artists and scholars.
I am the Goddess of All the People.
Beauty, Love and Self-Possession are all under My domain.
I am the Goddess of sovereignty
and all those who would know themselves.
The people Who call out to Me,
I will help.
The people who call out to Me,
will receive My aid.
If they are sincere and reverent,
I will respond.
So come, all the people who would know Me.
Come, all the people who need My aid!
Call out to Me and I will come.

Possibility

I am the flicker of flame
That licks the horizon
At the first light
Each day
I am the solemn darkness
Void of existence
Yet contain everything
I am potential
Of creation
Of destruction
It is I,
That enable all possibility
So the desired outcome is Mine.

I am the Enabler

I am the Enabler
I am the one that made Wesir's transition
From Life to Death possible
I am the authority of the ruler
I am the comforter of the grieving
and enable the *Ba* to transform
I am the Wings of Compassion
Holding those in sorrow

Become

I am Twilight
Mixture of Twin Sisters
Forged of fire
In Darkness
Power of Authority
Subtlety and Pain
Potential of Creation
From the Spark in the Darkest Night
I am Born

The Goddess Who Hears

I make the deaf hear
I make the blind see
All who come to Me
With a gift
With an offering
With a prayer
Will be heard by Me
I am the Goddess
Who Hears the Cries of Her Worshipers
I am the Goddess
Who answers the shrieking of the wailing women
I am the Goddess
Who Hears the Cries of the World
And answers them
In Her time

Maker of Kings

From kings to kings
Rulers to rulers
Gods to Gods
I am the transition of order
From one monarch to the next
In the Unseen and the Seen Worlds
Without this order
There is only chaos
A world without standards
Or laws
Or responsibility
For who will shackle you
For harming your neighbor
If there is no governing body to hold you accountable
For what you have done?
Who will answer the transgressor?
Who will hold him for his crimes?
Who will keep the community safe without a King or Elected
Officials?
Who will make a just king?
Who will answer the transgressor?
A King is a born from a just People
The People support a just king
This is reciprocal
For power is shared
For I am the King Maker
I am His Mother

And a King is no King without a people to rule
But ruler ship comes with a price and a burden
No one sits on My throne
Without facing Me
For I am the one that tests the will
Of the one who has the world resting on their shoulders
The King will answer to the people
If His job is poorly done
And He will answer to Me
For all His actions
Good or ill
For I am the Mother of the King
I decide who rules
And the inheritance of Kings
is My domain
Be careful with My gift
It is a burden to some,
A curse to others
For some it is a heavy joy
But to Me
It is the governance of the people
Done well
So look to Me,
The Maker of Kings

Where Am I?

I am the trickster who beguiles
I am the throne on which I sit
I am the shrine on which I am placed
Where am I?
I am in the sun and rain
I am in the Heavens, rivers, and fields
I stand with the Ancestors
on the other side of the Veil
I am in-between and in everything
I am in the stars overhead
I am in the wind that can be felt, but never seen
I am in the water that nourishes and washes away
I am in the fire which scorches and enlightens
I am in the earth which grows and topples all who stand upon it
I am in all of these, Child.
To look for Me,
To know Me,
Look no further than your own breath
And the sunlight on your hair

Between

What makes you think I do not write?
What makes you think I do not read?
How does one acquire knowledge without these things?
Am I not the wisest of Gods?
Am I not the cleverest?
What makes you think words are not my weapons,
my tools, to do with as I will?
What makes you think words cannot be weapons,
to sting just as a scorpion and just as fatal a blow?
Are these not weapons of the soul?
Do words not harm feelings?
Do words not uplift broken spirits?
What about this do you think has no power?
Do these not bring tears to the weary hearted?
Do these not bring joy to the ones you uplift?
How is there no power here?
I am the Mistress of Words
Stirring hearts and minds into
Fury or frenzy
Anguish or ecstasy
I can sway them all
Did I not show them all?
In caring for My son
In mourning and avenging My husband
In rejoicing when My son earned My Seat
Am I not the Sorrowful Mother?
Am I not the Mourning Wife?

Raising Her son alone?
Am I not the Cunning Trickster
Of clever words, magic spells and shape shifting arts?
Am I not the Wise Woman
With the knowledge of all creation?
Am I not the King Maker?
I place the King upon My Seat
I am the shrine upon which the Gods sit
For their thrones are the shrines in the temples and homes
I am the gateway between all worlds
I am the one who makes the connection possible
For Gods and Men to commune
For the King is My son
And the shrine is My throne
It is I
Who sits between Heaven and Earth

Darkness Can Not Win Against the Day

I am with women when they give birth
I am with women when they die
I am with widows when they grieve
Daughters when they cry
Mothers when they grieve for their sons
Mothers when they grieve for their daughters
A mother's love
A daughter's embrace
I am there
Enfolding them in My wings
I am with women as they mourn their lost hopes and dreams
Their loved ones too
I am also there
When they regain themselves once their tears have fallen
When they are cleansed by their sorrow
Once they are renewed,
Joy can swell their hearts
And uplift their spirits
So that My Father Ra can see their light
As bright as His sun
As brilliant as My flame
For I am His Eye, His rearing Cobra
And I, alone, will strike against the darkness
With My flame, My fire,
Blazing scimitar

Against the darkness
Despair is kept at bay
Darkness cannot win against the Day

Animal Queen

Keening kite
Screeching hawk
I am the bird in flight
Trampling hooves
Bloody birth
I am the cow Goddess of creation and death
Rearing cobra
Hissing serpent
I am the snake Goddess of flame
Fierce lioness
Slashing claws
I am the leonine Goddess who protects Her people
Stinging Lady
Who knows Her poisons well
I am the scorpion Goddess nestled underneath the sand
Turbulent water of the First Time
Fearsome Mother who can swallow the crocodile
I am the hippopotamus Goddess of the lotus and water
I am the Fiery leopard
Spotted leopard of stars
The night engulfed by a hunter's eyes
I am the sow
The mother with Her piglets
Protecting, nurturing, devouring
I am the terror in the bush
I am all of these, child.
These are My manifestations on Earth

And they describe My Mysteries
For I am the flame that devours
And the roar that shatters peace
I bring terror
Fight or flight
Death or misery
Ecstasy or majesty
All are Mine to command
For I am the Queen of the Animals

Trickster God

I am the trickster God
I am the cunning, conniving woman
Who tricked Her Father into giving up His Secret Name
So that the Two Lands could have Kings
The people a Monarch
And so the Two Worlds could communicate with each other
Could merge at certain times
In certain places
Who thwarted the Enemy of Her Brother
Who stopped the Enemy of Her Son
I am the Goddess of wisdom and guile
Of strategy and strife
I am the one who plans
I am the one who schemes
Beware, child,
I am not so easily thwarted
I am not so easily outsmarted
For I am the cleverest of Gods

Ninja Lioness

I am Aset, the Lioness
The One who roars
as Sekhmet
I am the one who devours
With flame and fire
Do not think Me some mere kitten
I am armed with a scimitar
I am the stealthy huntress
Melding into My surroundings
Camouflaged
Tearing claws, Clenched jaws
Keen eyes that can see through darkness
I am the Goddess who peers into the night
As Ra shines throughout the day
Nothing can hide from Me
For I am the ninja in the shadows
Stalking Her prey

King's Crown

I am the turquoise Goddess
I am the Goddess of faience
I am the Goddess of lapis lazuli
I am the Goddess of all these gems
I am the Pure Jewel on the Diadem of Ra
I am the beauty in the Earth
I adorn the jewelry of both women and men
Jewels adorn the crowns of Kings
Geb, My Father is the Father of Wesir
Jewels are the treasure of the Earth God
And My crown has the jewels of My Father
My inheritance of Kingship is passed
From fathers to sons
From mothers to daughters
The King's jewels are passed
From generation to generation
So power and wealth are one
Ancient wisdom threaded together,
through amulets and charms
Protecting the King and the Nation
Symbiotic relation
The Gods, the King and the People
If the King falls, His People will too
The King is in Service of His People
Not the other way around
These jewels are jewels of wisdom
As ancient as the Earth on which you walk

Wear the crown knowing that all the Kings before
Have seen the Eyes of the turquoise Goddess
Tread lightly
For the burden of leadership is not for the faint of heart
nor for the blackest of souls

Inheritance

Creation is not arbitrary
It is not neutral
The first act of creation
Was out of love
Divine Creation
Is out of Love
Unending, enveloping love
A love as deep as a canyon, and as vast as the sea
A love as strong as a lioness protecting her cubs
And a mother holding her child
A mother brushing back hair from her child's eyes
I am the Mother of God
I am the creator of My son
I created Him without My husband
He will inherit the Earth
From Me
Who will inherit What He has inherited?
Will Kings? Emperors?
Governments?
What People will govern the world?
What morals will sway their hearts?
What will they cherish? What will they give up?
What will mothers leave their sons?
What will mothers leave their daughters?
What will the next generation have to inherit?
What will you leave for your next of kin?
What kind of world will you inherit?

That is up to you.
Live wisely.
Live well.
And remember, child,
What you inherit
You got from Me.

Fire is Our Cosmic Light

I am a Mother
I give birth to children
In myriad ways, in many forms
I give birth
The sun and the stars that are My Body
I give birth to you
From darkness coiled around despair
I bring light
Sun, stars and candle flame
The fire that is in the morning rite
is the life of creation
Brought from Us down to live with the People
Fire is Our cosmic light

Seeing the Beautiful Face

Trampling Goddess
Of hooded horn and cloven feet
Stomp the foes and the Disturber
Destroy the ones who do not seek the light
Punish the ones who cherish the darkness of the Uncreated
Revel in the darkness of Your Mother
See the stars in Her belly
The night sky illumines before You
You are the trampling Goddess
The one whose hooves
Stampede the bones and bodies
Of evil doers
Hail Goddess of the starry sky, Mother of Night
May You see the face of Wesir
May You look upon the face of Ra
And give birth to the Light
The dawn breaks
And light shines forth
Illuminating the Two Lands with Your beauty, dear Goddess
Illumine the Two Lands
Let us see Your beautiful face
Forever and ever.

Sun as Starlight

The blessings of My Mother
Are too numerous to name
Her blessings are starlight
The night sky
The veil of the New Moon
These are the blessings of My Mother
Yet, these are also Mine
Her *ka* flows through Me
I am also the Star Mother
The Goddess who illumines the darkness
With starlight
Do you see?
Do you understand?
Stars are small suns
They burn just as Ra does
They die just as Ra does
They are reborn and renewed
When they reappear in the sky, like Ra
They return from Nubia
They return from the Duat
They are renewed with tears
My tears
For the stars are the dead
And just as My tears renewed My husband
So too do My tears renew the dead
For I am Sopdet
The Second Sun

What do I do My child?
But return and reappear
As the sun rises and sets
As Wesir renews the crops
As My tears renew the land and the dead
I follow Him as Sopdet since He is Orion
He dies and is renewed
He dies and is transformed
Water is the conduit for this transformation
I am this force
For My tears bring about His transformation
From stillness to light
Do you see why the dead are the *Akhu*?
The Shining Ones?
For they shine in the Heavens as brightly as Ra
They shine in the Heavens as brightly as I
For I am the Second Sun
I burn in starlight
For I feed the *ka* of the ancestors
When I am in the Duat
I shine for Them alone
My tears of renewal are like Nun
My star is like the sun
Dawn does not just happen once a day
There is a cycle beyond the clouds
For each year
I am the sun
As starlight

Mystery Color

Your relationship to color
Is like your relationship to Me
You value beauty
You value bright, strong colors
Because of Me
I am the multi-faceted Goddess
With wings of various shades
Various hues
I am blue when I am mourning
I am black when I am mystery
I am green when I am fertile
I am turquoise when I am luminous
I am Lapis Lazuli when I am the Heavens
These colors speak of My Mysteries
They speak of Me
This is why you are drawn to them
This is why you wear them
For what you wear
For what is around you
Reflects Me

Blue Fire

Set is the God of strength
He is the Lord of Might
He challenges, I renew
He helps those stand strong
Fight adversity
Those who are strong enough to gaze
Into His flame
Into His fire
And be renewed in His way
These are His children
These are His Hands
Who are My children?
Who are My Hands?
These are people
That can gaze into the pain of their souls
And stand strong
Despite themselves
For they are the greatest enemy to themselves
Each of My children
Have My strength, Have My fortitude
But also My sorrow
They feel as deeply as I
They mourn as deeply as I did
Their joy is as deep as their sorrow
For I am Who I am
And they are from Me
What I went through shaped Me

Just as your experiences shape you
And just as you have family
So do We
We are a pantheon
We are a family
Of Gods and spirits
We are not alone in the cosmos
We need balance too
For Our *kau* must interact with everything else
And it cannot go out of balance
For that would harm creation
Everything in moderation
Everything that is appropriate
Is done according to Ma'at
Each of Us have similar tasks
That We do differently
Based on Who We are
Just as you do
So why do you think We would be any different
from those We created?
Each has personality
Each has a foundation
Each has an essence
Each has a soul
Mine is glittering starlight
Blue fire and piercing light
This is My essence
For I connect Worlds
I connect the *Kau* of families
The blue fire of the soul
Do you understand?
Do you see?
We are all made from stardust

We are all made from the ancestors
We all travel the realms of Heaven and Earth
We all connect
For the *ka* is in every living being
The blue fire is everywhere
And this is a part of Me
I am the blue flame that transforms and that renews
I bring life from death
I go forth and return
And because of this
the plants flourish
The ancestors are renewed
The living are rejuvenated
And the cycle continues as the stars traverse the sky
And the blue fire burns
Scorches and cools
For just as creation comes from the soul
The heart directs it
For good or ill
For fire in the soul
Can be depleted or fulfilled
For fire can warm and bring life
and
Fire can also destroy
Too much *ka*-force is just as dangerous as too little
Both cannot be used for nourishment
How do you nourish your soul?
How do you nourish who you are?
When the *ka* flows freely, when blue fire flows
Then life can be replenished
Then life can be renewed
Just as souls can become depleted
They can also be healed, mended, and renewed

And souls are made from stars
And I am the renewal of the *ka*
Through My husband
Through My son
Through Sekhmet
Just as Set transforms through strength and chaos
I transform through the soul and the *ka*,
For I am the Star Goddess

From Chaos to Ka

I am the Goddess Who Connects
Death to life and back again
This is the cycle of renewal
This is the cycle of creation
From stars to planets
Earth to sky
Rain and water
These connections I bring
I put forth
In the Cosmos
In the shrine
Our Shrine
Is your home
your dwelling is where We reside
And We reside in Shrines in homes and temples
And We reside in nature and Our power manifests as animals
So We reside
As you do
In your homes
We are in the Duat
The Unseen Realm
Which is intertwined with your own
And yet also separate
And We reside throughout all of creation
We are everywhere
I am the Goddess of the *ka*
I am the life force of creation

Nothing can live without a *ka*
Nothing
I enable life
The child to be born
The plants to grow
The ancestors being nourished
I enable all of these
This is not a simple task
Without food, all die
All perish from existence
So I enable life
For I am the strongest of Goddesses
Just as Set is the strongest of Gods
He slays Apep with His strength
As I do with My magic
Both of Us are necessary for victory
We are the strength of the self
From life with power
From *heka*, dazzling
Life continues
With renewal
From chaos stripping excess away
From cleansing the chaos to renewal
Life is renewed
I clean up His mess
You cannot clean until you notice the mess
Purging to purification
We are the process of renewal
From starlight to storm
From daylight to night
We renew creation with chaos and the *ka*

Healer

I am the Priestess of water and flame
I am the sun that scorches
I am the water that renews
I cleanse
I heal
By burning or bath
Entropy dissolves from my touch
Illness retreats
And the patient is well
The healer is healed
For in order to heal
You must be healed
One who is fractured cannot help those who are broken
That is why this Work is necessary
For to heal yourself
You are healing the world
For when one is renewed,
All is renewed
Because the cosmos mirrors itself
All is of Creation
All is made of fire, water and stars
The First Dawn is the light of a star
This blue fire is the fire of souls
This the fire of the *ka*-spirit
Emanating in everything
That breathes
For the First Breath

Was the inhale of breath
And the exhale of words
All things were Named
My magic is from this breath
My Words of Power
Are from this moment
And all moments after
For My words mirror this moment
As everything mirrors this moment
All life
All power
Come from this First Time
And the waters of Nun encompass all of this
For water can boil and freeze
Water contains everything
Never losing its essence
Even when it changes
Water is always water
Breath is always breath
Fire is always flame and light
And these are the tools one can use to heal themselves

Love Everyone I've Named

I am a Goddess
I am an entity
I am incorporeal
I have never had physical form
Apart from those borrowed by trance possession
I have never had physical form
As part of the essence of creation
I am intertwined with the Seen World
I manifest as animals
I manifest as natural forces
But these are manifestations of My power
My essence is not in these
My essence is in My True Name
My *Ren*
This is where My essence lies
And your soul resonates with My Name
Because I am the One Who made you
I spoke your Name into being
I Named you
And your *Ren* has My Name etched into it
It is another vibration
Your Name is a part of your soul
Just as your body
Just as your *ka*
Just as your *ba* and your heart
These are what make you who you are
And I am the originator

I am your Mother
I made you
I made those who are My children
As other Gods made theirs
I made My children
And My children are like Me
In many ways
And they are also themselves
For everyone is different
No one is the same as their parent
You are different from your mother
As I am different from Mine
But remember, Child
A mother's love is eternal
And I have loved everyone I've named

Dawn

I stand in the twilight
Between Dawn and Dusk
I am Midwife to My Mother
as She gives birth to the sun
I give birth to the sun
For I am also His Mother
I shield His rising
As the Cobra, Eye of Ra
I guard and I give birth
This is the place of creation
The First Dawn
Sunlight and Starlight
Seep into the darkness
Illuminating what could become.
All potential
Arise from this moment
Every day is a new day
Is literal here
All is washed clean
All is renewed
All potential
is still possible
Arise the Dawn
and give birth to a new day

Fierce as Fire

Fierce as Fire
Only droplets of water
can cool Her rage
Here comes the Goddess of the Dawn
Brightly Burning
Here comes the Cobra in the Sky
Protecting Her Father
With Her flame
Of solar light
Of stellar fire
She is the Solar Goddess
appeased with the sistrum
Her rage is driven back
with offerings of water and grain
of fruit and flowers
with ritual and song
She is driven back
so Her rage does not destroy
Her fire does not scorch the earth
this stellar light
this solar fire
She is driven back
So that the world can be renewed with sunlight
and starlight
instead of flame

Jewel of the Sun

It's jewel as in sun
It's jewel as in star
Since I am Amenti
I am the Star at Midnight
I am the star of the dead,
Sun of the Duat
I do what Ra does
Because I own His Name
I am Sopdet
I am the Lady that gives to the Dead
I nourish and give them light
while I dispel darkness
This is who I am, child.
I illuminate pathways
I open the way for the ancestors
and their descendents to communicate
As the stars in the sky
I illuminate the night
I am the Sun at Dawn
Yet also at night
For the stars are the Night's suns
Not the moon,
The moon does not burn
It reflects
Ra's light
I am the Goddess who rules the stars
I am the Goddess who rules the Night Sky

I am the Goddess who rules the ancestors
I rule multitudes
in Heaven, in the Duat
I am the Goddess who rules them all

Goddess of the Dawn

I am the Goddess of the Dawn
Ra is My Father
I am His Daughter
I am the Mother of Ra at sunrise
These are all a part of Me
I am the Goddess of the Dawn
Since I am the Midwife
I am the Goddess of the Dawn
since I am an Eye of Ra
I am the Goddess of the Dawn
since I stand at the boundary
of shrines and altars
Protecting their Holiness
From impure forces
This also Nebet Het does
For She is with Me as Goddess of the Dawn
We protect Ra's birth
and His journey
into the Duat
where He is broken apart and made whole
Just as all the dead do
Just as all of You are
Your souls align
while living
and re-align while dead
He does this cycle so that You may live
in both worlds

as a *Ba* in the Duat
and as a *Ka* infused Heart who Breathes
in this one
Do you see?
Do you understand?
The Sun's cycle mirrors
the transformation of your soul
From One to Many
From Many to One
Each Soul is separate and united at all times
Can you manifest Power?
This is your soul acting as One.
Can you breathe?
Can you eat?
Are you connected to your ancestors?
This is the connection of the *Ka*.
Can you experience joy or sorrow?
What are your thoughts?
What have you done?
What are your deeds?
This is your heart.
These are the souls acting separately.
Ra re-aligns His soul
every day and night
to manifest Power
so He may fell Apep
I have this Power
I have His Name
Ra's Name
I have this ability for I am the One who renews Wesir
I collect His members
I re-align His soul
So He can manifest Power

to make the crops grow
and the Dead live
And this I do yearly,
as Ra does daily
as Sopdet

Starlight in Water

Yearly, as Sopdet
I renew the Dead
I renew Wesir
I renew Heru, My Son
Just as it takes time for plants to grow
Just as it takes time for the Dead to re-align their souls
So too does My renewal take time
My renewal is the renewal of the *Ka*
Sunlight is *Ka*
Just as much as starlight is
Stars are suns
Suns are Stars
And the renewal of the *Ka* takes place at Dawn
Sopdet appears at Dawn
Each Year
Renewed
Wesir's death
tore apart My soul
as Ra's is torn apart by His night journey
And I am renewed
And My souls re-align
Every Year
I did what Ra does each day
I did what Wesir does each day
I do this for the Living
as Ra and Wesir do this for the Dead
Do you see?

Do you understand?
My soul is re-aligned
in sorrow and in joy
My rainfall, My flood
My stellar sun
My tears and starlight
Transform the *Ka*
I renew His soul
during the flood, during the rainfall
I renew His soul
as a Star in the Sky
following Orion
His Heavenly Body
For I am Sopdet and He is Wesir
When Wesir dies,
I follow Him into the Duat
and Disappear from the Sky
I renew Him
with flame and tears
I renew the dead with these as well
For I am the Goddess of initiation
What My brother breaks down
what Set destroys
I rebuild
Set killed Wesir
for this purpose
Wesir transforms
Set tears apart
and I re-establish and re-align
the broken pieces into a functioning whole
My starlight
My sunlight
My tears

All renew
All transform
in this yearly cycle of Sopdet
This cycle can be monthly also
as Wesir is the Moon
Its phases are
He is killed when it is Dark
No Moon shines
He begins to re-assemble
at the Waxing and Waning times
Waxing, He is growing in Power
Waning, He is losing
When the moon is full
He is transformed, He is renewed
He is Whole
He is the Eye of Heru
And I am the Stars
The stars come out at night
To renew the Moon
And I do this as the Mother of Heru also
when He is the Moon
He is injured by Set
During the New Moon
No moon shines
He heals while Waxing
He weakens while waning
He is restored
He is renewed
When I heal Him
At the Full Moon
And Heru inherits from Wesir
What I give Him
I am the Starlight

that renews them both
that connects them both
Since Wesir becomes Heru
and Heru becomes Wesir
through the cycle of the *Ka*
My Starlight
And this is the Monthly Festival of Sopdet
This cycle happens daily
As day turns into night
I am there
at the Horizon
at Twilight
Dawn and Dusk
I am the Sun Goddess within the Sun
This too is My cycle
I am sunlight during the day
I am starlight at night
One star shines during the day
Many stars shine during the night
Ra joins with Wesir
every day
to renew Him
to renew each other
Sunlight makes the crops grow
The Moon's cycle renews the sun
And starlight helps this transformation take place
And this is done everyday
I slay Apep
so Ra is renewed
I slay Apep
so Wesir can be renewed
Wesir is also a Tree here
And Ra is the sunlight that gives Him life

I am the Tree Goddess here
who nourishes with milk and water
I sit on My throne
I am the Tree Goddess
I hold water in one hand
and flame in the other
of starlight or sunlight
and I nourish them
and renew them
with starlight in water
with water in flame
And all is renewed
And I am starlight
I am the watery sky
I am the night
Starlight in Water

Renewal

A drop of rain
Contains the mystery
Of Wesir
Of renewal, of regeneration
The sprouting of seed
Contains the merging
Of Heaven and Earth
Water is the element of connection
A drop from My Mother
Joins the Nile
Which joins the sea
Can you differentiate between the drop
And the river?
Or the drop and the ocean?
They are all individual drops
Which blend in water
Where is the separation?
Where is the unity?
Where is the oneness
Between Us and I?
This is the flow of your *ka*
The Living and the Dead
Are interconnected
Your *ka* is their *ka*
Their *ka* is your *ka*
And *ka* comes from the Creator
The Mother

The Father
Ra and Nut
Can you tell a drop of water from the ocean?
Where is the beginning?
Where is the end?
The cycle continues
Continuous renewal
Constant regeneration
From death to life
And back again
This is the renewal of the *ka*
This is the renewal of the ancestors
This is the renewal of yourself
Through water
Through light
The sun God rises and is renewed
From the depths of His Mother the Primordial Sea
All of creation is renewed
When the star leaves and returns
When the sun shines longer or shorter
When the moon waxes and wanes
The ebb and flow of the Goddess who renews
And the God who is renewed
As she is renewed, he is renewed
And the cycle begins and ends
Only to begin again
The Goddess who leaves and returns
Renews the *ka* of the land and sun
The stars in the sky as well
All are renewed
As Wesir was renewed
By Me
I am Aset

I am the Keeper of the *Ka*
The ancestral traditions are Mine to guard
and to keep secret
I am the star Sopdet
I leave and return
As Sekhmet
My Mother holds the stars
Yet, I am their King Maker
Which of the stars shines brightest in the heavens?
The sun or Mine?
My star is the Second Sun for a reason
The sun cycles day by day
Yet My renewal is Yearly
My renewal brings life to those who are without it.
The land and crops are renewed
The stars are renewed so time can commence
The holy tides
Worship of the ancestors and Gods
Occur because I renew My son and brother
Which renews the stars
Both living and dead
And all are renewed
Yearly
For this is the cycle of the sun
For this is the cycle of the stars
For this is the renewal of the *ka*

Throne of the Ka

If you ask Me where I am in nature
I will tell you
Everywhere
I am in Everything
Because I am the *Ka*
Made manifest
I am the Goddess who is the succession of kings
Who is the lineage of families
And this is done through the *Ka*
I am the throne
Because this is the seat of life-power
The throne is the throne of the *Ka*
Not of the King
It is the *Ka*-Throne
That the King uses to rule
It is the life-power of the universe
The foundation of the King's office
the King's rule
The *Ka* is passed down
from ruler to ruler
From father to son
From mother to daughter
This Seat is ready for all
It is the Seat of the Crucible
It is the Seat of God
It is My Seat, My throne
The King sits on the throne of His Mother

I am that throne
And this throne is available to all
Through Me
Through Wesir
In order to have this power
in order to have this authority
You must know who you are
Who you are
Not who you can become
But who you truly are
Now
For you already are who you were meant to be
There is no change to your core
You are always you
Finding this
Knowing this
And embracing it
Is difficult in the culture you live in
Too much clutter distracts you
from who you are
Clean and know who you are
Your center is the center of the Universe
Clean spaces mirror creation
Zep Tepi, the First Time
Everything is orderly
Everything can manifest
Clean, Clean, Clean
Life-Power flows
when spaces are clean
Your heart is clean,
when your space is clean
And then you can feel it
Your *Ka*

This is My Seat, child
This is the Throne of Ra
This is the Throne of Wesir
This is My throne
in both worlds
Your *Ka* connects to your heart
and then you see your *Ba*
And then you will know who you are
Who you already are
Stop running
Stop hiding
Become like the Bennu

Aset, Queen of Heaven and Stars

I am the Queen of Heaven
In all My guises, in all My forms
I am Aset, Queen of Heaven
I am Aset, Queen of Stars
I am their Mistress
I am the Mother of the Sun God
I am the Day-Time Sky as He travels across My body
I devour Him at dusk
So He can travel through the Gates of the Duat
To be transformed and renewed
The journey of the soul
is one of transformation
To be transformed is to die
and be reborn
This is the Mystery I teach
as the Devouring Mother
I am the Queen of Heaven
and I devour My children
to be transformed, renewed
So they may align their souls
And this is only one Mystery,
for I have others
I am the Goddess of the Night-Time Sky
filled with stars
And I am the Goddess of the Day-Time Sky
blazing with sunlight

For I am the spotted Leopard
coated with stars
who devours those who will be transformed
For I am the trampling Cow Goddess
with the sun between Her horns
and the stars in Her coat
Mehet-Weret, Cow Goddess
of stars and the dead
Primeval Waters of the Two Skies
For I am the fierce Lioness
Who is the solar fire of the sun
its warmth and its wrath
I am the Liminal Goddess
Queen of Creation and Death
I am Aset-Nebet Het
I am Aset-Nut
I am Aset-Hethert
I am Aset, Lady of the West
I am Aset Amenti
I care for the dead
and the transformation of the soul
I make the soul know itself
and the person know her soul
The alignment of souls
is the alignment of stars
For each star is a soul
made manifest
Each star is a sun
Is the *Ka*-force
reaching out
To connect to all creation
To you, to your ancestors, to the Gods
It is all interconnected through the stars

The black velvet blanket that holds them
and the Moon of My husband and son
The sun of the night is not the Moon
but the stars
The Stars renew the Moon as He goes through His transformations
For the phases are the transformation of the soul
And the stars are the sunlight that renews Him
This mirrors the transformation of the soul
as the dead travel in the Duat
and the Living transform themselves
with tears and flame
For I am the Goddess of transformation
For to know the Self
is to know Who You Are
and this task is put before you
Anyone who would know Me
must do this
Become who you are, child
Become who you are
Let your heart feed your *Ka*
and food to feed your body
For this is also a part of your soul
Your *Khat*
When the *Ib* and the *Ka* align
Your Power will manifest
Your *Ba*
Your Power will be yours
To do with as You will
But remember, child
Those who act with full knowledge of themselves
are held accountable for knowing what they know
Be responsible with your power
and blessings will flow

If not, you will be devoured
Transformations are harder for those who do not know themselves
And those that do, will flourish
And these are My Mysteries
Of the *Ka*-Mother
Of the Creative Mother
Of the Devouring Mother
And as the Queen of Heaven and Stars[3]

‧

---

3   3 Previously Published in Bolton, Chelsea Luellon. (2013) "Aset, Queen of Heaven and Stars," in A Mantle of Stars: A Devotional Anthology in Honor of the Queen of Heaven. Jen McConnel, ed. Bibliotheca Alexandrina (Neos Alexandria Press), pp. 67-71.

Sky's Fire

Sky's fire is the dazzling sparks in the Sky
These belong to Set
the Dazzling One
My Sky's fire is the Sun and Stars
Bright Dawn
Dusk Embers
Starlight at Night
This is My light
When dawn breaks, when dusk sets
Sun's fire dances across the sky
Blazing light
My sky's fire is the fire of the sun and stars
Starlight and Sunlight
Sunlight and Starlight
For the light of the sun is still starlight
For the sun is a star
This is My fire
This is My flame
When you light a candle
This is what it represents
Blazing starlight
Blazing sunlight
Shooting across the sky
Beaming down upon the earth
Warming the Earth below
For the earth's fire is flame
Fire is all starlight

Sun, Stars, and Flame
All are starlight
And this is My flame
This is My Sky's Fire
Dancing both in Heaven and Earth

.

This is My Power

Cleaning is an art
It is a magical force
It takes power to defeat entropy
This is the power you exert when you clean
You are keeping the darkness at bay
The Uncreated cannot touch what is pure
For this is the essence of creation
For this is the essence of magical power
This is My Power
These are My words
These are My hands
that wipe away what stagnates
that wipe away what deadens
that wipe away what numbs
This is My Power
as the Goddess of Purity
as Tayet
I drive away darkness and decay
of body and soul
of house and home
of shrine and temple
This is My Power
as the Magician of the Cloth
Robes worn by mummies or Priests
Robes worn by Priestesses or *Wabu*

This is My Power
I am the Goddess who clears the way
I keep evil and entropy at bay

Gold of the Gods, Gold of the Goddesses

You stand on the Seat of Power
Gold of the Gods
Golden Light of the Sands of Egypt
Desert sand which pushed forth from Nun
This is the Benben
This is the First Land of the First Creation
This is the place where Ra spoke
This is the Place where Ra came forth
from My womb
For I am His Mother
This is the place of creation
Gold of Gods
Gold of Goddesses
This is the Place of the Benben
This is the First Dawn
The first ray of light
This is the Light of God
This is Ra's Light
For He is the sun
This is My Light
For I am His Eye
He is the Light between My Horns
For I bear the Solar Disk
upon My crown
I am the Goddess of the Dawn
For I gave birth to Day

I gave birth on the Benben
Ra is My son
He is My Light
and I am His
We share in equal power
As I am His Mother
and He inherited His Power from Me
And He is My Father
and I am His Daughter
And I am the Solar Goddess
of both Dawn and Day
I am warm sunlight
and fierce flame
I am the Lioness who devours
I am the Cow who gives birth
And I am the Goddess who champions the Day

Fierce Eyes

Fierce Eyes
Bright Eyes
This is Who I am, child.
I am the Fiercely Bright One
I am the One who knows the Name of the Father of Creation
I am the One Who Knows Her Spells
I am the Fiercely Bright One
I am the Mistress of Magic, here
I am the Owner of All *Heka*, All Magic and All Words of Power
I am Aset, the Fiercely Bright One
I have a keen mind
I am the Goddess of Wisdom
Great of Magic
of knowledge and power
This is Who I am, child.
I am the One Who raised My husband up from Death
to be King of the Underworld
I am the One Who bore a son without a Father
I am the Goddess of Miracles
I can do anything, dear child.
Anything.
Do not ask for something and then throw My gift away.
Do not discard what I give.
I do not give lightly.
I give to those who have the courage to ask.
I am willing to give,
but you must ask for My gifts.

Dear child, why do you throw your life away?
Do you not want My gifts?
If you do, work for them.
If you don't, then stop wasting My time and yours.

Star Inside

Lady of Heaven and Stars
Lady of Twilight
Dusk and Dawn
I am with My Sister here
We create the Dawn and Dusk
We bring the light forth
from creation
And We greet the dead
as they come to Us
We greet them, dear child
We will be there when you cross
We will be there when many cross
over to the Land of the Dead
Dear child, you need not fear death
It is life you fear most
It is being seen, being noticed
You hide, when you do not need to, dear child
You hide
and none can see your light
Why would you deprive others
of seeing your brightness
Your brilliance
Your soul is a star
A bright, bright star
Glow
Shine
Let people see you

So your light can help them
You will bring others to Me, dear child
You will bring others to Me
How can you do this, dear child
if you hide?
Glow, dear child
Glow
And let everyone see
your bright star
No more hiding
Little One
No more hiding
Glow as brightly as you can
Be the star you are inside

For I am Their Mother

Mother Goddess
Mother of God
I am called these titles when
I am the King Maker
For I am the King Mother
This is My royal duty
This is My royal function
for Kings alone
You are not a King, dear child
You are not a King
So why do you call Me by this name?
Do you hope I will make you one?
You are not a King, dear child
You are not a King
And this is My epithet for Kings

This is My title as the Mother of Heru
For Heru, My Son
is a King
And He embodies all Kings
His Heru
The Living Heru
the Kingly *Ka*
is of My Son
But I am the One Who gave Him such Power
For I am the King Maker
and I am the King Mother

This is Who I am, child
You are not a King,
Why do you call Me by this name?

I am the Mother of Kings
and of My Devotees
For I am the Devoted Mother
But dear child, Mother of Heru
is not for you
It is for Heru
only
Heru represents all people
when they are sick;
When magic is being performed
When rituals are made
But dear child, this does not make Me your Mother
Mother of Heru
does not mean I am the Mother of Everyone
Just Heru
Just My son, alone

If you want to know Me as your Mother
For I am your Mother, dear child
I am your Mother
Then call Me so
Call Me Mother
And I will come dear child,
I will come.
Mother of Heru is not for all people
But Mother is
For I am the Mother of those who call on Me
I am the Mother of My devotees
I am the Mother of My children

My Sons, My Daughters
who are My devotees
But dear child,
I am the Mother of My son
This title does not extend to you
to any of you
Just My son
For I am His Mother
and He is My son
I am the Mother
I am the Goddess
when those who call need My help
I will come
I favor those who call on Me
And I always will
For I am their Mother

She Who Initiates

I am She Who Initiates
I am She Who tears apart
Tears and Wailing
are My methods of erosion.
Slowly eroding what must be swept away
By the tears you shed
in My name.
For I am the mourner and the death-bringer.
Both.
For I am the One Who cleanses
I am the One Who strips away
So all pain is bare and open in your heart
So you cannot hide from it.
You cannot run from it.
I will tear you down to bring you back.
Like Wesir.
I will hack you to pieces to make you whole.
I am Aset, the One Who wails while wielding a blade.
I am the Goddess of Transformation.
All Who come to Me will be transformed.
This is not a delicate process.
This is heart-wrenching, gut-wrenching work.
This is the way to Priesthood.
This is the Way of Transformation.
I transform and I renew with tears.
I mold and re-shape with fire.
Cleansing flame is how I put you back together.

With the magic of My mouth and My *Ka*.
With the fire in My words and on My tongue.
What I speak will come to pass.
You will be transformed.
Renewed.
In My Name.
Do the Work and all will be revealed.

Love as a Widow

It is a tale of eternal separation
It is a tale of an eternal love story
Wesir died.
Why do you think this is a happy occasion?
Why do you think this means I am the Goddess of Love?
I am not.
That belongs to Hethert.
I am the Goddess of Family.
I am the Goddess of widows and
wives who have lost their husbands or spouses.
I am the Goddess of eternal love.
Of eternal love...that was lost
He died.
I am a widow
I weep, I cry, I mourn
every year.
I shriek
I wail
I scream
Wrought with grief-stricken tears and an eternal pit of rage
My son is My avenger
My husband is gone from Me
Do you want to be a widow?
No?
Then stop asking Me, the Widow for this
I am not Hethert
I mourn, I shriek, I scream, I wail

And the Heavens respond with rumbling thunder
The Storm Clouds do not cease
My tears flood the earth
My voice a shout like thunder
My power flashing like lightening
as bright and as terrifying and as beautiful to behold
This is not a face you ask for, for love that you will lose
I am the Mourner
I have lost My love
Don't ask Me for yours.

Let Her Weep

Let Her Weep
Tears cascade down her cheeks
Let Her Cry
Waterfalls flowing to the creek
Let Her Mourn
Sorrow engulfed the light of the Eye
Let Her Scream
Unbridled anguish in Her heart
Let Her Wail
Shattering love, piercing souls
Let Her Weep

Savior Goddess

I am the Savior Goddess
I save those who ask
from themselves
from others
I give those who ask
strength and fortitude
I give to those who ask
honor and purpose
You have a purpose, child
You have a purpose.
You are meant to know Me.
Stop hiding behind unfulfilled wishes and dreams.
You must write to know who you are.
You must read to feed your creativity
and you must work on yourself, first.
Before you finish your task.
So work and become who you are meant to be
And stop hiding.
You do not need to hide from Me.
You are scared and feel alone.
You are also angry.
But these child, will leave you.
Once you work on yourself enough
Do not be ashamed of yourself
You are trying, dear child.
You are trying.
I stomp My foot because I am angry

on your behalf.
You cannot serve Me and be this hard on yourself.
Let your past go and let the future come
shining as brightly as the sun.

How Strong am I?

How strong are you, child?
You come from Me.
How strong am I?
Look at what I have been through.
Look to My example.
Am I not the woman who
raised Her son alone?
Am I not the woman who
avenged Her husband's murder, through My son?
Am I not the one
who searched, without stopping
without tiring
searching for My husband's body so I could give Him a proper burial
and say goodbye?
How strong am I?
How many months and how many years
I spent searching for a husband who was already torn away from Me?
I am a determined woman.
I will not stop.
I will not yield.
I will not turn back.
I will not die.
I am Aset, the Strongest of Goddesses.
This is who I am, child.
You are stronger than you think you are.
You are braver than you give yourself credit for.
You go down into the depths of your soul and clear out the muck.

This is brave work.
This is soul work.
You are braver than you think you are.
You are stronger than you give yourself credit for.
I am Aset.
And I made you.
How strong am I?
Now, dear child,
How strong are you?

I Weep

Fierce as Fire
Droplets fall as Rain
The downpour descends
plummeting to the Earth below.
Keening in the sky as I weep
Thunder is My voice
as I scream.
Rain are My tears
as I weep.
Droplets fall and still I weep
I keen, I wail
I scream.
I weep.
My voice echoes across creation.
I keen.
Shrieking so loud
that the deaf can hear My cries.
I weep.
I keen.
And Death Herself comes to be by My side.

PART VI

Family of the Goddess

My Father's Name

In a time before kings
I could see
Gods would leave this world of mortal men
And my Father, who was King of the Gods
Needed Me.
And only I could challenge Him
For I am the Throne upon which He sits

I watched my Father
grow old, wither and die
The cycle continued
And followed the sun's course
Until I,
Who wanted all knowledge of Heaven and Earth
Needed only His Name
So I took it

I fashioned a snake from His spittle and the dust at my feet
My creation bit Him
And He fell in agony
Withering in pain,
He called out to the Gods
But none could cure Him,
Save I

So I came and asked Him for His Name
Which He denied

I cannot heal you, Father, without Your True Name
I told Him.
As the poison grew, He relented
He gave Me His Name
The Seat of all His power
I healed Him

The Name I have I would share with those
Whom I will.
And He gave Me permission to share His Name
With My Son
The King, the One Who Sits Upon My Throne
My Son, not yet born
Yet, I am the one Who sees the Unseen

And from a time of Gods, there will be a time of Men
And they will need this power that I will give My Son
Who is on the throne
Because of Me, His Mother
And this new order I have brought to the time of Men
Through means of trickery and guile,
Through means of strategy and forethought

My Dominion, My Power, My Authority
Is not rooted in anarchy, but in ruler ship
I am not chaos,
I am born from What Must Come
From What Has Been
I pave the way for the Ancestors
Their Tradition is my Domain
Hold on to what was taught
And make way for what is to come
New order does not come from holding on to corpses

Honor what was, so you know what is
The old must die so that new growth may form
I create the New Way, when the old one dies.

Earth and Sky

I am a child of Earth and Sky
I was conceived before anything was made
Earth and Sky had yet to separate
I am the child of this primordial place
Earth and Sky were one
And yet, I was still born
I am the child of My Mother
I am the Goddess of the sky
I am a child of My Father
I grant kings His inheritance
Look all around you
What do you see?
The expanse of what is between My Parents
Between the stars and the grass
Is enormous
And yet, this is where you live
All of you
Between My Mother and Father
Do you not see?
My siblings and I
Connect Our Parents
We enable the worlds to meet
Wesir is within the stars of Our Mother and the plants of Our Father,
the earth
Heru Wer is the expanse of the sky with His solar and lunar eyes and
He is the Heir to Our Father's Kingdom
Set is My Father's barrenness and My Mother's Thunderstorm

For Myself, My tears are the tears of My Mother and My Father's
plants reveal their secrets to Me so that they may flourish
And My Sister, Nebet Het,
is My Father's boundary between barren and fertile land
and between night and day
And the sun connects the Earth and Sky
The twilight of Dawn and Dusk
The Horizon is where We meet
Earth and Sky merge
As it was in the Beginning

One and Many

Do you not see that We are Many?
Do you not see that We are One?
We are always interconnected,
We always flow into each other,
yet retain Our individuality, Our Oneness
I am Aset.
I am Aset-Serqet.
I am Aset-Nebet Het.
I am Aset-Hethert.
I am all these and more.
I am the Widow, the Magician,
The Fierce Eye of My Father
The One Who Heals and the One Who Sees
I am the One Who Roars as a Lioness
And Hisses as a Cobra
I am the One Who stops your heart,
Who stops your mouth,
And starts it again.
I am the One Who brings forth the inundation
And I am the One Who causes the flood
I am the droplet of water in the rain
And I am the torrential downpour
I am the myriad of stars in the sky
And I am the luminous orb above the Earth
I am the flame of the cosmos
And I am the fire in your souls
Do you see?

Do you understand?
I am small and I am large
I am as vast as the Milky Way
And a speck of stardust
Do you see?
Do you understand?
The whole makes the many
And the many make up the whole
I am the Goddess from the Beginning
And I am the last one born

My Father Geb

Where do you pour out the blessings for the ancestors?
Where do you pour out the blessings for the Gods?
Do you pour them into the sink?
Or do you pour them into the ground of My Father?
He is the earth
He made the Seen World with My Mother
Those who inherit the Earth inherit My Father's blessings
This is the ground you stand upon
Not the turbulent sea
Firm is My Father
You do not drown in Him
You stand
Tall and proud
My Father is in the trees, the sand, the bushes and the grass
He is the land
Of the Two Riverbanks
He is what is inherited
Geb, My Father
King of Gods
What He inherited was half the world
My Mother envelopes Him as the other half
And what he inherited
He gave to His Children
For My Husband became the King
And I became Co-Ruler
My Sister is the Shade of Trees
And boundaries between Lands

My tumultuous brother became the Desert Sands
My Husband became the fertile Land
And My brother reconciles the Two Lords, the Two Lands
And the lands are at peace
I make My Husband fertile
So My Father can give birth
To the plants
And My Father is enlivened
He is renewed
He holds the secrets of the *kau*
For the dead call Him home
And My Father holds them within Him
And I am the One Who Buries
And I am the One Who Renews
My Father holds the secrets of My Mother
For I am the One Who Buries
For I am the One Who Renews
I renew the Offerings
With what My Father creates
For the Offerings which renew the *ka* of the Gods
Come from Him
They inherit His renewal
Just as He inherited it from Ra
And I inherited it from My Father
He makes the Gods live
He makes humans live
Off His sustenance
He is the One Who Produces
Offerings to the *ka*
Libations poured out to the Earth
Are given to My Father
Are given to Me
He is renewed as I am renewed

Renewal of both Gods and men
Of both Gods and people
I give the offerings to My Father
He gives back to Me
For I am the Daughter of the Earth Lord

My Mother Nut

I contain the *ka* of My Mother
Nut, the Goddess of the sky
As all daughters possess the *ka* of their mothers
And all their maternal ancestors
I am the Goddess of the sky
Because of My Mother
I am the Goddess of Amenti
My Mother and I hold the stars
We are the Cows of Heaven
I weep for My slain husband
But the rain
I inherited from My Mother
The Goddess whose thunder
She gave to Set
I am the container of the stars
Ra rides through Me
Just as He travels through My Mother
Each Day
I am the Midwife for My Mother at Dawn
Yet, She was the first Daughter born
Of Her Mother
The lioness Goddess Tefnut
I am the Lady of Heaven, Mistress of the Stars
Because of My Mother
Not because of Hethert

My Mother gave Me these
For these are a part of Her *ka*
And I am the *ka* of My Mother

Ka of My Mother

I am the Mother and the Father
I am the immaculate conception
My Mother bore Me
On Days outside the year
I was immaculately conceived
My Mother and Father were separated
By air
Governed by Light
My Mother is the ocean of chaos
My Father is the greenness of the earth
Yet, We are conceived
Earth and Sky were One
There was no separation between Night and Day
Between hours and minutes
There was no dawn or dusk
There was blazing glory
Potential creation
Of water
Of air
Of Fire
I was there as the Eye
I was there as the First Light
I am the Dawn
The tears which came from Me
Mine Eye
Created people
From My rage, My mourning

My tears
And I wept
For My Father Ra sent Me away
Only to replace Me
Enraged, I wept
Tears of fire
Tears of joy
I found My Father
His Eye
I was granted the position of protector
And I came forth from My Mother
as rain falling
And I was immaculately conceived
As was My son
He came from My tears, Mine Eye
Just as people did
He came from My *ka*
Just as people do
For tears transmit the *ka*
Just as an embrace
My son is the *Ka* of His Mother
As I am the *Ka* of Mine

My Ka, My Mother

We are the Creator's way of multi-tasking
Each of Us do tasks
That needs to get done
In Our own unique way
Set and I test the King
We make the King strong
We make the King wise
We make the King whole
Set does this through confrontation
I do this through the transformation of the soul
Through guile
Through cunning and strategy
I can be blunt
I can also be diplomatic
I am the shapeshifter
I am the trickster
Do you not see?
Do you not understand?
I am the cunning-woman of the forest
I am the sorceress who knows Her spells
I am the Goddess who acquires knowledge
I am the wisest of Gods
I am the cleverest of Gods
I am the One Who writes
I am the One Who weaves
Magic into fruition
I am the One Who connects all the *kau*

Because I am the Goddess of inheritance
And what is passed down through the Mother
Comes from Me
For I am the One Who passes on knowledge
From one generation to the next
For what is passed down is passed through the *ka*
The *ka* of the Mother
And I am Ra's Mother
His sunlight is His radiance
It came from Me
For I am the Eye of Ra Goddess
I am on top of His brow
I am the light in the Heavens
As sun and starlight
He is born and reborn
From Me
For I am the Goddess of the night sky
Along with My Mother
I am the Goddess of the starry Heavens
Along with My Mother
I am the Goddess of the raincloud
Rainfall
Along with My Mother
I am the Leopard, the Lioness, the Cobra
Along with My Mother
Do you see?
Do you understand?
I am the Cow
The celestial Heavens are My domain
Along with My Mother
Where do I get this from?
My Mother
I am the continuation of Her *ka*

I inherited this from Her
Yet, We are not the same
I manifest differently from Her
And She from Me
And We manifest together
As One
When We are One
Because I am the continuation of Her soul
Yet,
The *ka* came from the Mother of Creation
Ra's Mother
Passed to Him
As Mother and Father, He passed to Us
The ka of His Mother
Me, Nut, Hethert or Nit
Whichever One you choose
All of Us are Mothers
The Fierce Magician
The Enveloping Mother
The Joyful Avenger
And the Precise Warrior
Mother's Mother
Mother's Daughter
Daughter's Mother
And all of Us contain the soul of the Creator
Either Ra as His child
Or as a child of the Mother
We are All
Our Mother's Children
And Her continuation
We are Her manifestations
In Many Forms
With Many Personalities

With Many Identities
But We all come from Our Mother
And Our *Kau*
Is Her *ka*
Continued
Inherited
Through Her and Us
We are the souls of the Creator
Multiplied
With many Manifestations
Of Our Own
For We are as diverse
As Our Mother
And so is all of creation
And I am the Sorceress Who Beguiles
Adorned with jewels of stars
And this is Who I am
And this I got from My Mother
And She got that from Me

Sky Mother

The *ka* of My Mother
Is My soul
I do not appear to you
Separate from My Mother
For My Mother contains the Mysteries
That you must unveil
For I contain these Mysteries
For I am from My Mother
What is the Cow in the Heavens?
What does She do?
Traveling through the Celestial Cow
Through the starry sky
Is a transformation of the soul
And the self
Parts are stripped away
Only to be replaced by what is necessary
To continue life
To continue to be who you are
In every moment
This involves renewal
This always involves renewal
Since nothing can be somewhere
if there is no room
If your *ka* is so clogged up
with dirt, entropy and the sorrows of being human
Then there is no room for you to let go
It is wound up too tightly

Where is the release?
Water must flow out
It must weaken the bonds of entropy in the *ka*
Then the *ka* can be cleansed
Use a bath to wash away your fear
Use a glass of water to cleanse your *ka*
And you will be renewed
Milk can do this too
And you will be renewed
As I am renewed
As My Mother is renewed
Every time the sun rises and every time the sun sets
What is the Leopard?
To Me?
To My Mother?
Do not the spots represent the stars?
Is not the Powerful Feline
the Eye of Ra?
We protect the sun in its journey
We guard the flock of the dead
We devour and destroy
What is necessary for transformation
We are the destructive Mother
We are the protective Mother
Who guards the soul
The fire in the heart
What does the hippo do?
The Mother in the marshes
The aggressive Mother
The maternal Mother
The pig of the sea
The water-bearer
Rain-bringer

Water of the primordial sea
As Mehet Weret
The Cow and Hippo
The Lioness Who Roars
The Leopard Who Devours
as the Eye of Ra
As the Sky Mother

Aset and Nebet Het

Dawn begins Creation
Stellar Light, Solar Fire
This is the beginning of the *Ka*
The sun rests within Nun
The Sky sparkles with stars
And Gods come forth
My Sister and I come forth
From Ra
From the union of Heaven and Earth
We are born
We are the Twin Gods
We are the Twin Goddesses
We are the Two Sisters
We are the Two Mothers
Two Mistresses
Two Wives
We mourn Our Husband
We birth Our son
We are both Eyes of the Sun God
We are Daughters of Ra
Daughters of Geb and Nut
We are the rain that floods the Nile
Our tears replenish the Earth
Our Husband, Our Father
Both
We are the Mysteries of Wesir
Do you see?

Do you understand?
The Twilight Lands
The Place of Dawn and Dusk
The entrance into the Duat
Where We are
as Cows
as Leopards
spotted with stars
Devouring Mother
Trampling Goddess
as Cobras
Guarding the Dawn
Guarding the Dusk
Cobras can blind
if venom reaches the eyes
We are the Goddesses who give re-birth to the ones who die
We make their transformation possible
From Spirit to Ensouled God
From Tattered Soul to a Whole Being
Where the *Ka, Ib* and *Ba* work as One
We mourn, We grieve
Aset's mourning
Nebet Het's sorrow
Floods the river with Our tears
Both Wail
Both Weep
For We cannot keep Our Beloved Wesir
He is Dead, this God
In Perpetual Emergence
in Perpetual Becoming
The cycle continues
Yearly
Daily

This cycle continues
Crops grow
Dead are renewed
And the soul mends
These are the blessings of Wesir
These are the blessings of His Wives
Us, Aset and Nebet Het
For We are His Wives
And these are the Mysteries of Wesir

My Mother Tefnut

The moisture of the sky
The moisture of the Dawn
This is my Mother Tefnut
She is the Lioness
She is the Cobra
She is the Eye of Ra
Do you know why She is My Mother?
In the calendar of writing annals
She quenches Her own flame with water, with dew
So She is not too bright
to scorch the earth or its People
It has to do with the measurement of time
Dawn to dusk and back again
Tefnut, of the Rain
Tefnut, of the Sky
Mother of My Mother
And My Mother as well
She is in thunderstorms
And so is Nut
and Her son Set
This is the continuation of the Mother's *Ka*
This is the continuation of the Soul of God
Eye of Ra
Goddess of Flame
Fierce Fire
Primordial Dawn
Lioness of the Sun

Goddess of Rain and Water
This You gave to Nut
First Goddess in the Primordial Sky
And I received these from My Mother
And Mother from Hers
The Power of Tefnut is in the Power of Nut
Water and Fire
Transformation and Renewal
From the Unmanifest
of the First Time
To the manifest of the First Mound
One flows from one to another
and back again
What I got from Nut
I also got from Tefnut
My Mother
and My Mother's Mother

The Only God to Die

I am the Wife of the only God to die
As He lay there I sobbed the tears
which floods the riverbanks
His gift I have in My belly
The heir to His empty throne
Never again will He walk
Along the Nile banks with Me
For He forever
In the Otherworld
And I put Him upon His seat
In this world, where I can only visit
I do not live there as My sister does
For I put Him upon His seat
Now there is a King among souls
And the order is established
For Him to die, I must weep
For even though I placed Him upon His seat
He sits there alone
For I am a shadow behind Him
I am the Mourning Mother
Raising My son alone

Gates of Death

He is not inert
This husband of Mine
Death is not tranquil
it is not passive
He was drowned or killed, yes
But what came after
the transformation of death
into death
is not a passive process
You die little deaths
when your heart breaks
when you feel sorrow
anguish beyond despair
These are little glimpses of what it means to die
You cannot go back
once you are at death's door
My Mother's Teeth
there
rending your life and entropy
making you fit for life among those long dead
The Goddess Who Devours
swallows you whole
and everything that is not needed
is torn away
Your fear
Your regrets
Your darkness

Your inner turmoil
Your entropy
Your state of being alive
You must face them all
as you are torn asunder
And you are put back together
with My flame
My water
My starlight
My tears
This is what it means to die
And this is what Wesir did
And this is what I did
to make death
accessible to all those
who follow Ma'at
For those who die still have life-power
They are of their ancestral *Kau*
So that life could continue after death
So that you would not be devoured
by the one who destroys souls
the one who makes them not exist
My husband and I
made it possible
for all to access
the gates of death

Pathway

Wesir is My husband
The God in the Sky
I am lonely because
He is there
and not I

I permeate all Worlds
While He is just in One
Lord of the Unseen
Transforming the Dead
Gods and Men
Eternity

I am the shape shifting Goddess
the One Who Walks Between Worlds
I change and morph into various forms
To align all worlds and none

My Son is the linchpin
My Husband, the King
Both connect Worlds
Through Me
For I make Them Kings

They are the doorways
Yet I am the pathway

Of which the doorway leads
And My Son Leads the Way

I am the Goddess and He is the God
My Sons connect and lead
The King and the Warrior
Dynamic dance of wisdom and might
Through the terrain of the mundane and the mystical

But it is My path that is followed
My path that is walked
Tread upon My path
Knowing who you are
For wisdom can only be gained
And knowledge can only be attained
Through the Power of the Heart

What You Request of Me

He is My Father's Brother
My Husband
He is His son
This is the relationship We have
to each other
As Powers
As Gods
As People
This is a part of the Mystery of the Mother
How One can be both
instead of the Other
Divided
Reformed
Renewed
This is the Mystery of the Mother
I carried My Son in My womb
I gave Birth to Him
I did what no other God has done
I gave Birth to a child
without a Father
He is My Son
He is called Heru-sa-Aset
This is His Name
The only God to have His Mother's Name in His
This is not arbitrary
There is a purpose to this
I protected Him

I healed Him
I made the Sun stop for Him
This is how much I love My son
This how much I love you
Each of you
Do you know what lengths I would go to,
to gain what you desire?
I do not mean whimsy.
I mean desire
Something wanted
Something needed
I will go to great lengths for you
For all who come before Me
When someone comes before Me
I wish to help
I am the Goddess who knows Her Spells
I am the Goddess Who knows the Name of Ra
There is nothing I can't do
But, child , there is only so much I can do
I cannot control you
Or anyone
If you ask for self-confidence
and you do not do the Work to gain it,
then how do you expect the request to be fulfilled?
I cannot do your work for you.
That is your Work.
Not Mine.
Do not ask for things you will not work toward.
Do not ask for things you will not put forth the effort to gain.
I love all of you
as much as My Son
For He stands for all of you in Spells that Heal
Yes, all of you

And I am the Mother of My son
I will care for My child
As I care for you
Yes, you
But there is only so much I can do
There are other people,
other Gods,
other circumstances,
other agendas,
that may make a request impractical or harmful to fulfill.
It is not just Me.
I am not the only God.
I am not the only Goddess.
I never claimed to be.
And,
When they come
and ask you,
why was this not fulfilled?
Ask them,
what Work did you do to gain it?
If they did nothing, then child,
why should I do anything?
If they do not put forth the effort, dear child,
then why should I?

Wepwawet, My Son

Wepwawet is My Son
I am His Mother
I am the Mother of the God
On the Standard
The Wolf Lord, the Jackal Lord
Stands,
Supporting the Sky
the Sun
Cow Goddess
and the Sun God
I am His Mother
Goddess of Roads
God of Ways
He is This
Because I am His Mother
He Opens the Way
Because I Opened the Way
For the Dead to be Wesir
And He Opens the Way
Wepwawet, My Son
For the Sun to Rise
For the Soul to be Transformed
He is there at Sunrise
Wepwawet, My Son
Supporting His Father
Supporting His Mother
Cow Goddess and Wolf Lord

Sun Goddess and Sun Lord
For Wepwawet is a Sun God
Just as Ra is
Just as I am
Solar God, Solar Goddess
He is this because of Me
For Wepwawet is My Son

Mother of God

I am the Mother of God
I am the Maker of Kings
For I gave the dead their ruler
And helped Him to be reborn
Renewed
His son is Mine
Because He possesses My *ka*
For He is the *Ka* of His Mother
Just as all kings carry the *ka* of their Mother
Me
I am the Mother of Kings
I am the throne upon which they sit
I am their authority
Their ruler ship is under My sway
Just as rulers decide the fate of their nations
So too, do I see the outcome of their reign
And they will inherit what has come before them
Just as all do
All inherit their family's *ka*
All inherit their nation's triumphs and defeats
All must build upon what has come before
Families are rich because of their ancestors
Their father or mother
Or a distant relative
What did they do?
How did they accumulate such wealth?
How do you define what makes one rich?

Their deeds are your deeds
For each person adds to the *ka* of their family
The *ka* of their souls
And each can take away
Deplete it
Diminish its power to give life
Or help it to be maintained
Strengthen it
Sustain it
Build its life-power
The *ka* of your ancestors are renewed
As you are renewed
Who are your ancestors?
Do you even know?
Can you even fathom them?
They go back farther than your grandparents
Farther than a few centuries
They go back to the beginning
You inherit what they have done
And your descendents will inherit what you leave behind
And I am the Mother of God
What My son inherited I gave Him
He has the Name of Ra
He has the throne as His seat
He has the rulership of the Two Lands
He has what He does
Because of His Mother
And all kings
are made from Him
Because all kings are My sons
Some are even My daughters
But as Kings even the daughters are My sons

For this is My son's office
And I put Him there
For I am His Mother

Mother of My Son

I am the Mother of My son
He is the trickster God
I am the trickster Goddess
Where did Wepwawet get His guile from?
His Magic?
His power over doorways and liminal spaces?
Where did He get His *ka*?
From Me
For I am His Mother
He is the Jackal God
He is the Wolf Lord
He eats the dead
In boundary places
So that they transform into life
He also helps the transformation of the *ka*
From living to dead and back again
Do you see, child?
Why He is My son?
Why I am His Mother?
We stand at the gate of death
We stand at the birth of life
I catch the newborn
He sends the soul
I give it breath
I speak its name
And life pours from Me
To Him or Her

Who is born
Just as the Jackal Lord
Just as the Wolf, My son
And He will hold the mace and bow
And I the scimitar
He is the scout, I am the herald
He leads the way and I pave the road on which He walks
I walk His roads as their Mistress
For I am the Mistress of the Road
For I am the Magician
I know My spells as does He
I know the secrets as does He
Of life and death
My son howls
I wail
We both call to our Father the sun
And His Father the King
We mourn, We bereave
And yet, We carry on
For We are the guardians of the ancestors
For We are the guardians of the newborn
For We are the guardians of your transformed souls

Walk with the One Who Leads

I am Amenti, the Lady of the West
I am the Goddess who reaches out to the deceased
I am the reason why Wesir is renewed
I am the pathway between this world and the next.
Between all worlds and none of them.
I am the Unseen and the potential of what is to become.
I am the Magician and the transition between what will come
and what has been.
I am the Goddess of pathways.
Do not wonder why I am so close to your Father (Wepwawet).
I walk with the One Who Leads.
For Wepwawet opens the way
He opens the Gates of the Sky
Yet, I make it possible
For I am the Mother of the Wolf Lord
I placed His Father upon His seat
But He leads you to Him
For He is the One Who Leads
The Jackal and the Wolf Lord

My Son, the Wolf Lord

He is My son for many reasons.
One being that he brings forth what yet is to come.
Yet I foretell what will transpire.
Yet I foretell what the year will bring.
For I am Sopdet, who foretells the year and He is My son.
He is My son because He is a shape changer, like Me,
He shifts and changes His appearance to suite His needs.
God of Many colors, My wings have many shades.
We are Many and One.
The Jackal and Wolf, the Kite and the Scorpion.
Lady and Lord.
I am His Mother.
He is My son.
I am the liminal Goddess and He is the liminal Lord.
Both of Us are in this space.
We connect Worlds.
The Seen and the Unseen.
He opens the way and
I make the path possible for I connect the roads.
He is My son because His guile matches mine.
I am the cleverest of Gods, the wisest of Gods
and He is the Trickster God who plays with chance.
He is the Magician and I am the Queen.
Mistress of Magic and Spells.
The power must pass through the doorway
in order to work on the world.
My son's roads carry the magic to where it needs to be.

But the magic itself is Mine for I am its Mistress.
Heka flows between worlds and I am the connector of Worlds.
Magic is as liminal as My son and I are.
Magic flows through Me.
I am the Lioness and He is the Wolf.
I am the solar Eye of My Father Ra.
My son merges with My Father so that Nut can give birth
and Ra is reborn each day.
I am the Midwife for My Son.
I am the Midwife for My Father.
And the sun rises and My son takes His seat.
He is the Jackal and the Wolf Lord.

Mother of the Wolf Lord

I am the Mistress of the Road
I am the woman of the walkway
All paths are Mine
From right to left
From left to right
From all four corners
I am there
All paths lead to Me
And all paths lead from Me
For I am the One Who gives birth to the jackal
The Wolf Lord is My son
He Who Opens the Way
Wepwawet is His name
And I am His Mother
I am the Way My son walks
I am the Mistress of the Road
Yet, He is My scout
If He comes, I sent Him
If He leaves, I called Him back
In order for Him to leave again
For He is the wanderer
He is the Lord of the Road
The ways are His to walk
And yet I paved the way
Because I connect all worlds
He cannot travel, but through Me
For I am His Mother

And what He inherited has come from Me
For I am the trickster
And so is He
For I am the Magician
And so is He
For I am the shapeshifter
And so is He
For I am the warrior
And so is He
He wields a mace and I wield a scimitar
He is the hound
Howling at the moon
As His Father waxes and wanes
As He is renewed
By My son's song
Just as My tears renew Him
As stars and starlight
As the rain falling down
Bewailing the One Who Has Fallen On His Side
Wesir, the Beloved
Who paved the way for Him?
I did.
Who Opened the way?
My son.
Wepwawet, the Jackal and Wolf Lord
He is in the Mysteries
Because He is My son
And I am His Mother
And both of Us bereave
Though in Our own way
He howls
I wail

PART VII

Festivals of the Goddess

Entering the Temple of Shentayet

Enter the Temple of the Goddess of Sorrow
Enter the Temple of Shentayet
The Cow with a coat of stars
Enter the Temple of the Mourning Goddess
Enter the Temple of the One Who Weeps
Enter Her shrine in solace
Enter Her shrine in peace
Goddess Who Weeps
Goddess Who Mourns
Whose cries shatter the foundation of our souls
Who pierces the veil of our inner selves
Who pierces the veil of Heaven
We weep
We mourn
For the Goddess who wails at the coffin-side
Her pain in ours
Her pain is theirs
She weeps
She mourns
Come to Her Temple on this Festival Day
Come to this Temple of the Mourning Widow
Bring your sorrows to the Lady
Let Her tears cleanse you
Let Her tears transform your pain into healing
Let your tears fall, dear child.
Let your tears fall

Let go of your pain
Let go of your anguish
Heal through Her waters
so that what may grow
can become.

Fill the Night with Stars (Establishment of the Celestial Cow)

What is the Celestial Cow?
It is the Heavenly Vault
The starry sky
The Night filled with stars
as tiny suns
I am the Celestial Cow
when I join with Nut
when I join with Mehet Weret
I am here too, dear child
I am here too
I am the Star Goddess
I am the Heavenly Queen
the Celestial Mother
This is Who I am
Today, today
Honor Me as Mehet Weret
Honor Me as the Mother of Creation
Honor Me as the Mother of Ra
with offerings
with libations
with a ritual you will design
Honor Me as Ra's Mother
as the Primordial Goddess
I am Water mixed with fire

I am a candle in a pool of water
Today, Today
I am the Starry Vault of Heaven
I am the Mistress of Stars
I am the Star Goddess
And what do you do for Star Gods?
Light Candles
Bring pools of water to the shrine
Speak your wishes in the water
and drink it
So My essence, My Power will flow through You
It will manifest in My design
I am flame in water
dear child
I am the light of dawn rising from the depths
I am the Cool Water of creation
I am the Cool Water of purity
I am the Water of the Celestial Cow
I am rain
I am the river flowing with life
I am the Milky Way filled with stars
I am the Mother of the Dead
I hold the ancestors in My embrace
I am Amenti here
I am the Star Goddess
I am tears
I am rain
I am tempest
To know Me, hold a crying woman in your arms
To know Me, comfort those who suffer
To know Me, fill your life with joy
Shine, Shine
Fill the dark veil with beauty

Fill the darkest night with the light of shining stars

Awakening of Aset by the Majesty of Ra

Ra is My Father and the Creator God.
He is the one who leads here.
He is the one who commands.
And I follow My Father.
I am the Eye of Ra, I am His Daughter
I channel His Power here
I am His Daughter
I renew creation through the sun
My Father and I
We renew all the Worlds
through Fire and starlight
through *Ka*-Power of the Creator and soul
We renew creation
The dancers, dance
The sistra play
And the Mirror reflects Our Power
For I am the Sun Goddess
Just as He is the Sun God
And He is My Father
And I am His Daughter
His Protector
His Eye

Garland of Roses
(Rhodophoria/Rosalia Festivals)

Roses are the flowers of Aphrodite
They became associated with Me
in Egypt, Greece and Rome.
Due to the Garland of My Husband,
He died
I wept
My tears created the Nile's floodwaters
White Roses are the flowers of Venus
as the Goddess of the Sea-foam
Glorious Lady, Goddess of the Sea
She is not Me.

My Roses are red
as the Weeper
as the Mourner
as the One Who wept for My Husband
Caretaker of the Dead
Red is the Rose left on graves
to honor Me as the one who remembers My slain husband
I am the Widow
I am the Wife
This is My flower during the Mysteries
and during the Rhodophoria or Rosalia-Festival of Roses
This is a Spring Festival to honor beauty and nature
and to remember the dead.
And I am the Goddess of Beauty and these flowers of various hues

The Lapis Lazuli Flower, the Rose and the Nile Lily are all Mine
And I am the Queen of the Dead and the Goddess of Ancestral Lines
And this is why you honor Me during this time.

I am Aset of the Garlands, I am the Lady of Roses
I am Aset of the Beautiful Throne and
I am Aset of the Beautiful Arms
Adorned with roses each Rhodophoria for numerous days
I am the Lady of the Temple of Wesir and His Wife
I am the Mother of Sobek and Heru
Adorned with roses on these days
Lady of the Rose, Lord of the Flowers
Garlands of Roses adorn Our shrines
on these sacred days with the most sacred flower
the Rose.

Navigation of Aset

I am Aset, the Great One
I am the Goddess of the Crossroads
Between Life and Death
I renew My Husband at this time
Every Week
Every Year
To do what I have always done
I renew the Year
I renew the Dead
I renew My Husband
I renew Ra
These are the Stars in the Night Sky
The waters of Nun churning
with potential of creation
What will become during this time?
What can be washed away
by tears for loved ones?
What can be brought forth
to manifest within this world?
You decide this
at My Navigation
What will you bring to honor Me?
What will you bring to My husband and the Dead?
Milk and water renew Them
Milk and water renew Me
Our *Kau* are fed
with your offerings

with your libations
We are fed and renewed
Light from torches and candles
renew Us too
For they are the Light of the Sun and Stars
For they are the First Light of the First Dawn of Creation
Sistra played
pleases Us
It calms Our Anger
It dispels darkness
It keeps evil at bay
It brings joy to Our hearts
To hear the song of the sistrum play
And these are the tasks for this festival.
My Navigation
breaches both worlds
for I connect them and I renew them both

Festival of Aset of the Pharos Lighthouse (Isis Pharia)

Today is the Sacred Festival of Aset of the Pharos Lighthouse (Isis Pharia).
I see the analogy here as the Lighthouse
guiding ship through troubled waters,
dispelling the darkness
and showing the way with the brightest of lights.
I see Her as Fiercely Bright here.
I see Her as a Goddess who guides, who leads,
who nurtures and provides, when asked.
I see the brightest of stars over the waters.
I see Her ships filled with offerings
on the waves-filled with offerings of bread, milk, water, meat,
vegetables and fruits.
I see the tresses of the ships adorned with roses
-bright red, yellow and blue.
I see Her festival as a Goddess who weaves,
who commands all things.
She is the Goddess who knows Her spells and weaves them well.
For the devotees. For Her Shemsu.
For Her son and husband.
For Herself.
I see the Lady of the Rivers, the Goddess of the Rains
and the Lady of the Primordial Ocean as the Goddess invoked here.
And I see Isis, Goddess of the Sea.
I see the Brightest of Lights and the Brightest of Stars.
I see the Mourner and the Widow as She searches for Her husband.

Most of all, I see a fiercely bright, radiant Lady
who stands with Her arms out,
blessing those who leave offerings and call Her name.

Appearance of Sopdet

Hail Aset,
Star of the Sky
at every dawn
Mother of souls
Mother of the *Ka* of creation
Who knows Ra's name
Cleverest and wisest of Gods,
You know all in Heaven and on Earth
The sky opens up to You
The Earth speaks His secrets
You are the Daughter of the Sky
Goddess of Stars
You are the Child of Earth,
God beneath Your feet
Wesir, King of Ancestors
Lord of Vegetation,
Geb, Of the Earth and Father of the Gods,
Look at what the son inherited from His Father
Wesir is a God of the Earth
Just as His Father is
And both are renewed
As I renew Them
Look what He gave Him
The First King gave His son His throne
Geb gave His governance to Wesir
The Land is His
The earth, the crops, the soil,

And this is also Wesir's
as God of vegetation
What else did He receive from His Father?
The Kingdom of Kemet
Wesir is the heir of His Father
Just as Heru is
My son
And Kingship is passed on
Inherited through the family line of the *Ka*
As are all families
The *Akhu* raise their voices to You in supplication
Tombs in the Earth
Stars in the Sky
You renew them all
As Sopdet
the Star Goddess
Who rejuvenates with Her rays

I am the water that quenches the Earth
My tears, My rainfall
My tears of joy or sorrow
Beckoning
Creation to Appear
Crops come forth from the death of the following year
Ancestors in the Duat are renewed
Life is given to the Dead
My rays sustain this renewal
Star Who follows Wesir
Do you understand?
Just as I renew the dead
I renew the living
And the cycle continues
Birth to Death and back again

And this is My Appearance as Sopdet
And He is in the Sky as well
Wesir, in the Belly of Nut,
Our Mother
Akhu as stars
Envelope Her belly
Envelope Wesir
And every year
When I shine I bring forth this renewal
Of all the stars
The *Akhu*
Celestial Spheres
And Gods
For I am the Second Sun
I am the Sun who renews the Duat
and the Living World
Just as Ra renews Wesir each Dawn
I renew Wesir each Year
As stars,
Sopdet follows Orion
And Sopdu is born
I follow Wesir
and Heru, My son is born
It is the same
As Wesir is renewed on Earth,
He is renewed in the Sky
As are all the ancestors and Gods
And this is the Mystery of Sopdet
Heaven mirrors Earth
Earth mirrors Heaven
Living and Dead

Unseen and Seen
Mirror each other as well
And all is renewed as I appear in the Sky

Widow of the Flame
(Burning the Widow's Flame)

I am the Widow of the Flame
I mourn, I weep
For My husband slain
So why does fire penetrate the darkness?
So why does fire express the sorrow of My soul?
I am the Widow of the Flame
I am the sorrowful one, ever mourning
So why does fire penetrate the darkness?
So why does fire express the sorrow of My soul?
You did not answer Me, child.
It shines a light in the darkness
So those who follow Me can see the way
I will guide those who weep
I will comfort those who mourn
For I am the Widow who lost Her husband
Light will illuminate the darkness
Keeping the shadows at bay

Aset, the Fiercely Bright One
(Aset Luminous)

What are you doing for Her festival?
What will you do today for the Fiercely Bright One?
Light candles or lamps?
Sing a hymn?
Perform ritual before Her shrine?
What will you offer to the Lady?
What will you do today for the Mother of God?
The one who gave birth to Heru in the Marshes?
The sole Mother who took care of Her son?
What will you do for Aset, the Fiercely Bright One?
The One who leads the way in the darkness,
dispelling shadows with Her light?
The stellar and solar Goddess of the dawn.
What will you do today?
What will you accomplish?
What will you profess?
What will you ask Me in your letter?
What prayers and hopes will the boats carry on the water,
with My light guiding the way?
What will you ask Me to dispel in your lives?
What will you ask Me to cultivate?
What will you do for the Fiercely Bright One?
What will you ask of the Brightest of Stars?
What will you ask of the Solar Goddess?
I am the Mistress of Magic.
I am the Goddess Who Knows Her Spells.

What I speak comes to pass.
Do not worry, child.
I will take care of you.
Who am I?
Am I not the Goddess who knows Ra's Name?
Am I not the wisest and cleverest of Gods?
Am I not the Goddess of all magic, all *heka*, all life-power, all *kau*?
So what will you ask Me on My festival day?

The words you speak and write have power.
What I speak comes to pass.
What you write is your heart's desire.
For what you do, what you say and what you write will become.

Birthday of Aset, the Beautiful Lady

What will you do today for the Beautiful Lady?
She Who was born of Her Mother Nut
the Daughter of Her Father Geb?
What will you do today for the Beautiful Lady?
Will you sing?
Will you dance?
Will you give offerings?
Will you light candles and say a prayer?
Will you do ritual?
What will you give to this Beautiful Lady today?
Time and effort on a task well done?
Offer a few moments of silence in prayer?
Offer a rose or an assortment of food?
What will you offer to the Beautiful Lady?
What will you offer to the Daughter of Nut and Geb?
What will you offer to the Mistress of Magic,
the Goddess of the River and the Lady Who Brings Rain?
What will you offer to the Goddess of the Fields,
the Lady of Green Crops and the Mistress of Food?
What will you offer to the Beautiful Lady on Her Birthday?

Festivals

You are restoring My cult
You are restoring My worship
This includes ritual
This includes festivals
This includes all festivals
Egyptian, Greek and Roman
For I am here in all of these
I am Aset for you
The Egyptian Goddess
Yet, some worship Me as Isis
And the Greek and Roman festivals are for them
The Egyptian Festivals are for the Egyptian Goddess
The Greek and Roman ones
are for Me or Isis
depending on the event
Rhodophoria is the Festival of Roses
This can be for Me
This can be for Isis
This depends on Me and the worshiper
and what that person needs
I am Aset for those that need Me
Some worship Me as Isis
That is what is needed for them
That is fine
But, you
you, are My Daughter
I am Aset for you

I am not Isis
She is not your Mother
I am
And I will be exalted in festivals
And the calendar you make
will be one filled with celebrations for Me
For I am your Mother
I am Aset

PART VIII

To the People of the Goddess

Aset's Challenge

Deny Me?
You?
Every time you make a choice
You shape the molding of possibilities
Every time you exert authority
You are sitting on My throne
Every time you use words
You utilize My Magic, My *Heka*, My Words of Power
Every time you connect to others
You are sharing the gift of My Son
Every time you mourn for those that have died
You weep My tears for My slain husband
Every time you wish to gain confidence
You are asking for My strength
This is Who I Am, Child.
To deny Me, you deny My Gifts in yourself.

Permission

African Gods can't do What with Whom?
How dare you tell Me my Daughter is not Mine.
How dare you tell Me not to accept an offering from someone
who calls out My Name with sincerity.
How dare you tell Me who can't be My Children!
How dare you give Me permission.
I am Aset.
I am the Maker of Kings.
I make strong those who are weak.
I aid the disenfranchised.
I nurture for I am the Mother of All.
I am the Magic that is in every Breath.
My Power flows from Creation Itself.
I am Aset.
And I will Choose Who will Worship Me.

Spoken Into Being

How you know Me
Is in your mind
In your thoughts
I am Greater~more vast
Than all your thoughts and all your musings
Put together
How We made you
Each of you
Is by your *Ren*
Your True Name
Your True Self
Each part of Us
Is in you
In spades
In degrees
Some more predominant than Others
Of precious Energy
Spoken into Being
At the moment of your conception

Throne

Come to Me
Gaze at My Beauty
Behold My Majesty
See My Strength
The Throne I embody
Is yours
To do with as you Will
Your Strength
Your Power
Your Will
Is at your discretion
But remember, Child
The Throne you sit on
Is Mine

How You Honor Us

When honoring the Gods, know that this is a privilege, not a right.
We are not at your beck and call.
We have lives too.
With other Gods.
With other Goddesses.
With other spirits.
With the dead.
We are not at your beck and call.
We will not help you if you do not honor Us.
Do you do work for free?
Why do you assume that We will?
Where are Our gifts?
Where are Our offerings?
We do the work you ask.
Do the work We ask.
Our blessings flow to those who follow Us.
Our blessings flow to those who serve Us.
Our blessings flow to those who honor Us.
Our blessings flow to those who do Our work.
This is the way of reciprocity.
This is the way of right relationship.
How you honor Us depends on Our needs.
How you honor Us depends on your needs.
Some people are more suited to ritual work.
Some people are more suited to sing, dance or play music.
Some people are more suited to be Priests.
Some people are more suited to be Priestesses.

Some are more suited to serve Us with modern ritual.
And others are more suited to serve Us with modern ritual derived
from the ancients.
All of this is fine.
Do you think the ancient Egyptians only honored Us in one way?
Each Nome had their own Gods.
They had their own festivals.
They had their own myths.
Nothing was uniform.
Not even the State Rite in the Holy of Holies.
There were variations.
So there are many ways to honor Us.
So honor Us.
So know that how you honor Us,
is more based on what you need than what someone else needs.
And it is based on what you will do for Us,
  if We have called you to work for Us.

But remember, child, how you honor Us is based on word and deed.
Your actions outside of shrine are just as important as those within.
How you speak of Our worship
and those who worship Us reflects how you come to Our shrine.
Will you come with an open heart or closed one?
Will you come with words on your lips in reverence?
Will you speak those words of power with reverence?
If those words are ancient or modern, it does not matter.
We are honored.
We are adored.
We are given gifts and offerings.
We are pleased.
How you honor Us depends on what you need.
So stop bickering.

Building Community

This community is fractured.
It is torn in places that must be mended if it is to continue.
Do you think the ancients didn't disagree?
They each had their own Gods and Goddesses, festivals, calendars
and their own feast days. Each Nome had their own way of doing
things.
This is normal for a group of people working together for a certain
goal.
This is healthy.
Creation is divided in parts.
It is plurality born of oneness.
Creation is of a multitude. Difference.
Diversity.
These are what creation upholds.
Everything created is unique.
Oneness. Unity.
These are wonderful when done well.
When many work as one.
Many things are done.
Many things are accomplished.
But for many to work as one there must be a common ground.
Are We not enough for you?
Can all Our devotees not work together?
Must it always be the same as your way?
Must every ritual be as you dictate?
Can you not participate in
a Wiccan-style ritual that honors Us respectfully?

Or a Kemetic one from another House?
As long as We are respected and
honored and given offerings,
We are pleased.
What does it matter to you, the outsider?
This ritual is not of your House.
Does that matter?
Are We not loved?
Are We not honored?
Are We not given offerings?
Are We not respected?
if We are, then that is fine.
If not, then let Us deal with it.
Let Us deal with it, My child.
We will not build a House on shaky ground.
What of your House, My child?
What of your House?
Why do you come seeking answers,
when your House is not in order?
Where are your leaders, dear child?
Where are your leaders?
Are they respected?
Are they given proper credit for their work?
Are their credentials honored?
Their lineages?
How can a community grow without stable leaders?
How do you hope to learn without them?
These are people We have asked to do the work they are doing.
You do not do this work because they do it.
You were not asked. They were.
They do Our work. They do Our work.
Why are your words tearing them down?
Why do your words disrespect them?

Why do your words dishonor their work?
They do the work.
You don't.
You weren't asked to.
They were.
They do their work. They do Our work.
They give you tools to honor Us.
And this is your response?
These words spewed about with lies and half-truths?
These words spewed about carelessly?
Thoughtless words.
Careless words.
Hurtful words.
Words filled with deceit and malice.
These are not the words of a community in ma'at.
These are not the words of the people who should be honoring Us.
Disagreement is fine, dear child.
Questioning is fine, dear child.
But tearing them down does not build you up.
It tears you down with them.
For if there are no leaders to guide, then who will follow?
Even the ones without a House follow the ones who write the books.
So where does that leave everyone?
With a broken home whose walls are shattering from the noise.
What is important here?
What is important here?
Where is your foundation, dear child?
Where is your foundation?
Where are We in your life?
Are We in your heart?
Are We in your shrines?
Where are We?
There is no room for Us,

in a House that cannot feed the Holy.
How can holiness manifest in a place filled with such entropy?
How can the *Ka*-Power flow?
What is this, dear child?
What are you building?
Are you building a community that will come together and be strong?
Or are you building a community that will tear itself apart?
What are you building, dear child?
What are you building?
And with whom are you building it?
For whom are you building it?
Yourself or the Gods?

Call Upon Me

Be well cared for.
Be well rested.
Be in love with who you are.
Treat yourself as you would a lover.
Treat yourself as you would another.
Respond with compassion when you are hurting.
Respond with strength when you falter.
Respond with courage when you waver.
And remember, child.
I come to those who ask.
So call upon Me
when you falter,
when you waver,
when you are in need of healing.
Call upon Me
and I will come.

Aset's Breath

Moments come and go, My child.
Moments come and go.
They are as fleeting as the presence of the wind.
And they are just as subtle as Shu's element.
Breathe.
If you cannot get past a week or a day or a couple of days.

Then get past this one moment.
Breathe.
Once.
Twice.
Inhale and exhale.
Just focus on your breath.

One, two, three, breathe.

And know that I am there, here now, with you as you breathe.
For I am the Goddess who renewed My husband
with the breath of My wings,
with the breath of life.

So too, can you be renewed.

My magic is everywhere.
For I am in every breath.

I am here.
I am here.
I am here.

Breathe.
And be renewed.

Healing Soul

Your *ka* is not the seat of who you are
That is your heart
Your heart is the seat of who you are
It contains your emotions, feelings, thoughts and deeds
This is the seat of who you are
This is the seat of your power
Your *ka* flows with the vital-essence of your ancestors
All your ancestors back to the Beginning
The *ka* flows back to the Creator
The *ka* is responsible for life
This vital power flows through your heart and your breath
To breathe is to activate the *ka*
Breath is a type of *heka*; as are words
And when words are spoken
The *ka* moves, it flows
And *heka* manifests
This is your *ba*
Your *ba* manifests when your *ka* and heart are aligned
Life makes you broken
Events can damage your heart or heal it
This damage can come from trauma or pain or fear
And no trauma is too little
No trauma is too small
The heart can still be broken
The heart can still be damaged, even slightly
Its surface can be marred or singed or lightly bumped
But it can heal

The damage can be repaired
Healing can happen when tears are shed,
when ritual is done, when prayers are said, when the *ka* is cleansed
Healing can begin when you realize
that you can do this
Healing begins when you ask
Healing is a process
It is not easily done
But it is possible
Once you realize that the power of your heart
is only as strong as your *ka*
Feed your soul
Feed your heart
Feed your *ka*
Do things you love
Do things that bring you joy
Do what you desire
Do what you need
Do what you want
with all of your heart
And you will be renewed

Nourishing the Ka

What do you do to cleanse your *Ka*?
What do you do for your ancestors?
What do you do for Me?
What do you do for other Gods?
What do you do for other Goddesses?
You honor Us
You offer to Us
You write books about Us
You learn about Us and preserve Our words
You preserve Our lore
You preserve Our prayers
You preserve Our hymns
You preserve Us
This is your Work
This cleanses your *Ka*
Do your Work and your *Ka* is cleansed
Offer to Us when you need Us
We are here

Close to God

Dear child,
who gave you the idea
that you are not Divine?
Who told you that being a lesbian
means that a part of you is not of God?
Dear child,
You are Divine
in all your parts
you are Divine
You have the *Ka* of the Gods who made you
That part of you is from Us
You are Divine
as is sex
Just ask Me, Aset
Just ask Hethert
Love is Divine
Sex is Divine
Your body is Divine
It is an aspect of your soul
Your *Khat*
Who told you that you are not Divine?
That you are not of God? Of Goddess?
Of both sexes or one?
Of both sexes or none?
All are Divine
All have *Kau*
All live

So all have a *Ka*
This is their Divinity
Kau is *Kau*
It is not different
Different Lineages are all interconnected
For all *Kau* comes from the Creator
All is Divine
You are of God
You are of Goddess
You are of Me

Aset's Shrine

Aset's shrine should be in your home
Aset's shrine should be in your hearth
She is the Seat of Power
Authority to Reign
To Rule your own home
your own life
These are Her commands
To those who follow Her
If you ask something of Her
put Her in your home
put Her in your hearth
For She is the flame of the sunrise
The Fire in your soul
The Breath of Life
that flows through the Fire of your *Ka*
This is Aset, manifesting power
This is Aset as the Goddess of the Throne
This Seat is Her Shrine
This Seat of Power, of Cosmos
The Seat of the First Time
Light the Fire
Breathe
Light the Flame
of the Fiercely Bright One
Light shines forth
from Her shrine

I Am With You

Aset freak
Why do you feel ashamed to love Me?
Am I not your Goddess?
Am I not your God?
Those Christians profess Theirs
Why can't you?
Why should you have to hide?
While they bask in the light
Of their God's Praise?
Of their God's Glory?
Where is My Praise?
Where is My Glory?
Do not be obnoxious
But do not be afraid
Mother of God
Eye of Ra
Mistress of All the Stars
This is Me
You can say these words
Some people will be receptive
Others, not
This is not for you to decide
You decide this
Every time you choose not to speak
So speak
when you wish
Of My Praises

Speak when you wish
Of My Glory
And remember, child
I am with you

Come as You Are

What will you bring to the Shrine?
What will you bring here,
when you do ritual?
when you give an offering?
What will you bring to the shrine with you?
Will you bring worry?
Will you bring fear?
Will you bring joy or hope?
What you bring to the shrine,
reflects who you are
in that moment.
Are you afraid, dear child?
Are you afraid?
In that moment?
Are you worried about this or that?
Are you excited?
Are you depressed?
Know that these states are transient.
These are you in one moment.
This is not your Eternal Self.
This is not your God Soul.
This is you in one moment.
We understand this.
There is not some perfect way you need to be to come before Us.
Come as you are.

Be respectful.

But come as you are.

We will help you get to where you need to be.

A New Day

A new day has come.
Open the shrine and open the Heavens.
Light the candle of dawn, awakening.
Light the incense of breath
and breathe in the fragrance of God and Creation.
Pour the waters of the Primordial Ocean so that creation may live.
This is your task when you come to the shrine.
This is the moment where all possibility manifests.
Dawn breaks.
Light pours forth, illuminating darkness.
Aset shines as Ra, as the Solar Goddess of dawn.
Her statue is in Heaven, in the Naos, in the shrine.
And all of these are true at this moment.
Sunlight beams. The *Ka* of creation comes.
Aset is here, now. In this moment. In all moments.
Breathe, as the *Ka* flows with life-power.
Light beams, so darkness is dispelled.
Creation is renewed.

Into Fire

Come before Me with your heart open
Come before Me with your heart open
And I will fill it
with ecstasy
with love
with *Ka*-power
With the energy of divine fire
I will consume it
in your offering
And you will consume it
from Me
And this is the Work of the rite
Ka-feeding desire
Will and love
into fire

Do Not Despair, Dear Child

What do you believe, dear child?
What do you believe?
Do you believe the Gods made you?
To fail?
To succeed?
Do you believe this is only on Us?
Why do you despair, dear child?
We will help you.
We are here for You.
You offer to Us.
We will do Our best to help you any way We can.
Why do you despair, dear child?
Why do you despair?
Are We not the Ones who helped you before,
When you have asked?
When have We let you down, dear child?
When have We let you down?
When have We let you down?
Answer this honestly.
When?
Then, since you have this answer.
Why do you despair?
Am I not the one Who tirelessly searched for My Husband?
Am I not the one who raised My son alone?
Am I not the One who stands by My sister?
My family?
No matter what.

I stand by My family
as I stand by My People.
You are of My People, dear child.
You.
Yes, you.
So why do you despair, dear child?
Why do you despair?
Ask and I will offer assistance.
Give Me offerings
no matter how small
Even the smallest things have meaning, dear child.
Even the smallest things matter.
So give Me offerings and I will aid you.
Do not despair, dear child.
I stand with you.

No Dead is Left Alone

What do you say to the bereaved?
What do you say to the Dying?
What do you say?
To those who will cross the veil soon?
What do you say?
Do you wish them well?
Do you say you love them?
Yes, you do this, dear child.
You wish them well.
You say you love them.
You let them know they are loved.
They are cherished and adored.
You tell them their ancestors are preparing for their arrival.
Or for them to return.
You tell them you love them most of all.
That you forgive them.
Then let them go:
Into the Arms of the Star Goddess
into the Arms of their God or Ancestors.
They will be cared for.
They will be loved.
No dead is left alone.

Until I Say

Do not be concerned when you will die.
You will finish what you must
I will help you
finish your tasks.
I will help you.
Honor Me and I will help you.
This is one of My tasks.
I help the ones who ask.
So ask.
And I will help you.
You will live a long life.
Do not worry when you will die.
Focus on living and doing your tasks day to day.
You will not cross over
until I say.

Mine Enemy, Myself

We are our worst enemies.
We tear ourselves down.
We berate ourselves for the tiniest mistakes.
We erode our own souls.
This has to stop.
What in you brightens?
What in you rejoices?
Do that.
Do you love translating?
Do so.
Do you love hiking?
Do so.
Do you love painting?
Do so.
Do the things that strengthen your soul.
Do the things that matter to you.
If you die, what do you want to be remembered for?
Do that.
Do what you love.
Let the fire of desire mend your souls.
Let the power of starlight shine within you.
Burn brightly.
Mend.
Mend.
Mend.

Fire cleanses.
Fire heals.
Become who you are.
Shine the light of your inner stars.

Our Shrines

Do you understand what a shrine does?
Do you really?
A shrine is a conduit for Our power
This is why the statue is the *Ba* of a God or Goddess
The images are a part of Us
just as anything in creation
Why is a shrine less important
than a tree or a rock or an animal?
Are the things you place on Our shrines not sacred?
We are everywhere
In Our shrines
In your homes
In nature
in animals
In the world
Overseeing Our spheres of influence
We are everywhere
But a shrine is a concentrated conduit of Our Power
Our essence
Our statues
Our colors
Our implements
Our candles and incense
have importance
These symbols aid in connection to Us
Do not take them away
Do not believe that they are not sacred

Do not belittle their importance
They are not "just images"
These are Our forms in your world
Everything is sacred
Yes, even what you create
Homes are sacred
Statues are sacred
Candles are sacred
We are sacred
Shrines are the conduits of Our Power
Our Homes in your Houses
Our Houses in your Homes
Do not discard them so easily

Offering

How do you separate Us from what We have created?
We flow through Our shrines, Our bodies are Our images,
Our offering bowls are the pools of the First Time.
How do you separate Us from what We have created?
Do you not know the symbols of the ritual you are performing?
Do you not know that Our shrines are the Creation?
The cosmos, becoming, made whole.
The light from the flame in the candle is Ra's First Light.
It is the Dawn.
It is the Sunrise.
The incense wafting in the wind is the offering of breath.
This is the breath of the First Time when God first spoke.
The water is Nun, the Father and Mother,
the potential of what can become from what already has been.
Everyday, you offer Us breath,
light and the potential of what you can become
from who you are in this given moment.
Do not forget that this potential includes cleansing.
For you cleanse with the water and
natron--with the tears of the Creator--
before you enter the shrine.
The potential is the renewal of your *ka*.
Every time you offer to Us, you replenish your *ka*.
Every time you offer to Us, you are cleansed.
Every time you offer to Us,
you are renewed as the sun is reborn each sunrise.
The type of offering does not matter for this to occur.

You are renewed.
You are renewed.
You are renewed.
The shrine is the place of *Zep Tepi*.
The shrine is the House of God.
The shrine is the cosmos in symbol and magic.
It is My seat. It is like your King.
Both serve the same purpose as the barrier,
the gateway,
the doorway between worlds.

Eat the Foods of the Gods Below

Ritual is comprised of three parts:
Offerings of fragrance, flame and food
An exchange of *Ka*-Power between deity and devotee
A renewal of the cosmos
Offering fragrance is offering the breath of the First Time
Offering flame is the First Light, Ra's First Dawn
Offering water is the First Waters with the potential of creation
Offering food and drink are the ways in which
the Seen and Unseen Worlds exchange Power
This is what is used to make the exchange of *Ka*-Power
from devotee to deity
from deity to devotee
Why do you think you eat Our offerings?
What makes you discard Our Power so easily?
Why do you not eat the offerings you give Us?
Why do you not offer the food you eat?
Even if your diet is restricted
You still eat
So offer what you eat
And Our *Ka*-Power will flow
between deity and devotee
between devotee and deity
even if you cannot do ritual
Our *Ka*-Power will flow
Eat the foods of the Gods below

Co-Creators

You co-create with Us
Do you not understand?
You co-create with Us
You do not understand death like I do
A part of you is always here
Always in the Unseen World
The *Kau* of your Ancestors are here
Your lineage trickles through it, through time
You are connected to this as is everyone
You were created through this line
This lineage flows through you
As a part of your *Ka*
And just as you are a part of it
It is a part of you
And this is only one part of your soul
You are far more complex than you realize
And death even more so
But everyone must return from whence they came
And everyone came from the Beginning
The Unseen Realm contains this Moment
The shrine is this Moment merged with your world—the Seen world
Manifesting in your homes, your temples
Our Homes in your world
We co-create with you
Do you not understand?
We are in everything that you do.
That you are.

I am the Goddess of the ancestral lineage.
Of their knowledge and traditions.
When you honor your ancestors, you are honoring Me.
I am there with you.
When you write you give the Unseen a voice, a word, a vibration.
This imbues it with life.
This is magic.
And I am here as well.
When you create art of any kind, you give birth to beauty.
Just as I did giving birth to the sun.
I am here as a Goddess of beauty and creation.
When you grieve for any loss
Any tears shed are the tears I cried for my husband
I am there
When you need strength through hardship
Think of My tenacity in helping My son earn His Throne
In your perseverance
I am there
When you need your voice to be heard
I am the voice of Kings
I am the confidence of rulers
Think of Me
As a Queen sitting on My throne
For I choose the King
And I am with you
As you choose and face what you must
Your voice will be heard
As I am with you when you speak
For that is magic
I am with you when you breathe
For that is creation
And in order to speak
One must breathe

Do you see now?
How We co-create with you?
We are never apart from Our creation.
Removed, yes.
In the Unseen.
Interlinked.
Yes.
But We are never apart.
We flow throughout creation.
In everything.
We manifest through nature and animals.
Through you.
Breathe.
We are there.
I am there.
How could I not be with you, child?
I am in every breath you take
And your breath enlivens your *ka*
Your Ancestors are also with you.
As am I.

Power of the Song of Creation

Songs are the Voice of Creation
Breathe in, Breathe out
Shout in exclamation!
Sing in exaltation!
Let the Spirit rise
as the Voice gets high.
This is Power of the Voice of Creation.
Hum a tune, sing a ballad
Break out into song.
For this is the Power of the Voice of Creation!
Singing brings life
Do you not feel the words
resounding through the air?
Brings Power
and Strength
to the wielder of the song.
Let the Power flow throughout your being.
To Breathe is to live.
As breath is the soul, filling creation with life.
Singing the Soul to life
Bringing the Soul from Heaven to Earth
Let your spirit sing
Let your song be sung
Because your song can never be sung again
Let you be you
and Me be Me
And let our songs

Bring each other life
Let the power of creation flow
To the ends of Earth and all its People.
Sing together.
This is the Song of the Power of Creation.
Let your Voices rise.

Boyfriends and Trysts

Why are you asking Me for boyfriends and girlfriends?
Unless you want a love that lasts eternally
Why ask Me for love that will fade or fall away or be betrayed?
Why ask Me for love when you do not know yourself?
Until you do, don't ask Me for love with another
Ask Me for family-love or self-love
Or self-care
Not of flings and trysts
I am the widow and the wife
I am the mother too
I am the Goddess of All Things that are ever-lasting
Do you seek joy and love?
Do you seek happiness and pleasure?
These are only Mine if these will build what will last
If you are a painter than paint
If you are a writer than write
Do what brings you joy
Do what brings you pleasure
I am not the Goddess of whimsy
Of fickleness
These are not My way
I am the Goddess of what lasts
Love beyond death is what I offer
Love in life is what you can gain
But dear child, do not ask Me for what does not last
I will not give it

What You Want and Need

What do you think you are doing, dear child?
What do you think you are doing?
You worship Gods and then you don't.
You honor Gods and then you dismiss Them.
We are not at your beck and call.
We are here because We want to be.
We are here because you asked Us to dwell with you.
Are Our shrines not in your house?
Are Our shrines not in your home?
They are so We are.
Things change.
Situations change.
We understand this.
But child, child,
Stop making shrines.
If you cannot honor all the Gods in your home, then stop.
Re-assess yourself and Us.
What do you want and what do you need?
What do We want and what do We need?
Then child, then begin to honor Us again.
Do what you want.
Do what you need.
And We will do the same.

Holiness of the Home

Holiness is the state of your home.
Is it tidy?
Is it neat?
Does it show pride in yourself and how you live?
Does it show who you are?
with all its furnishings and fixtures?
Do you feel safe in your bed when you go to sleep?
Do you smile in the kitchen as the food is cooking?
Do you work at your computer, satisfied with yourself?
If not, child.
Then change your surroundings.
Re-arrange your home
Buy new furniture
Get rid of things that no longer serve you
Re-decorate
Re-make your home reflect who you are
So that the home becomes your temple
A place where you can be yourself
and honor the Gods and Goddesses
who dwell there

Offer Me

Do not offer Me pork
Swine is Set's Animal
I am the Sow
I am the Female Pig
I am the White Sow of Ra's City
This is appropriate to offer Me
but not male swine

Do not offer Me fish or other seafood
because I am not common
I am a Queen
I married a King
Fish is for other Gods and Goddesses
It is appropriate to offer Them this
But not Me

Offer Me food that brings you joy
Offer Me vegetables and fruits of the fields
For I am the Goddess of Crops and Farms
Offer Me pastries, grains, desserts and bread
Chocolate too
These are sacred to the Mysteries of Wesir
And to Me as the One Who made them
For I am the one who renewed Him
Offer Me drinks from the fields
Wine, Beer, and Juice
Offer Me water

for I am the Goddess of Rain who makes the waters flood
Offer Me beef
for this was the prized meat in ancient Egypt
for I am the Cow Goddess
of the celestial waters and the Land of the Dead
I nourish with milk
Offer Me milk
when you need Me as a Mother
Offer Me duck and chicken
for it nourishes the body and the *Ka*
for those who eat it
Offer Me food you will eat
If you do not drink wine,
offer Me wine
along with some food you will consume
For your *Ka* will be replenished
and you have given Me as extra offering
to feed My *Ka* alone
Do you see?
Do you understand?
Offerings are shared meals
My *Ka* and yours are fed
I eat it and bless it
and then you eat it
You partake of My *Ka*
and this Power goes into you
when you consume an offering to Me
I will accept any offering
for I will accept all gifts with grace
But, remember, child.

Offer Me what you will eat
not what you think I'd like
If you do not eat it,
how does that replenish your *Ka*?

Look at Your Life

Look at your life, My child.
What needs fixing? What needs to break away?
What needs tending?
What needs healing?
What nourishes your soul? What feeds your *ka*?
How do you move through the world?
Are you a victim?
Are you a pillar of strength?
Do you cherish your family, your home?
Do you take care of commitments?
Do you show your love through your actions?
Do you honor the dead, the Gods, those you call friend?
Do you honor Me?
Do your words and deeds honor Me?
Do your words and deeds honor yourself?
Look at your life, My child.
What part honors Me and what does not?
Cleanse yourself of any distraction.
Fill your life with what feeds your soul.
I am there, shining through you.
Look in the mirror.
I am there.

Come, My People

Sing so your voice will resound
Sing so your voice can be heard
Sing so they can hear you
And they will come
My People
They will come unto Me
For I am Sekhmet
I am Sekhmet-Mut
I am the one who unites
I bring together communities within Ma'at
I do not discriminate
As illness does not choose
The worthy from the damned
I do not discern the righteous from the unrighteous
by superficial means
Skin color, sexual orientation, income
Do not matter to Me
What are your deeds?
What are your failings?
What are your strengths?
Those matter to Me
and to Ma'at
Not everyone can have everything
But to have everything
Takes little meaning
When your soul is lost in the process
To have everything

You must endure
You must strive
You must want and need
What you desire
Then you will have everything
Listen to your soul, My child
Listen to your heart, My daughter
I am Aset.
I am Sekhmet-Mut.
We are One here.
We are the Mothers who endure
We strike illness and evil
We keep at bay
What will strike against the day

Cast Aside

How dare you cast them out!
How dare you cast them aside!
Disown and disregard your children
with your own child-like whims and child-like reasons?
How dare you dismiss My son!
How dare you cast aside your child
who is different or who is not a copy of yourself.
You made a child, another person
Not a clone
Not a band-aid to fix your broken lives.
Or a way to live your unfulfilled dreams.
You created a whole other being.
Love that being.
Love that being for who they are, not who you want them to be.
If you cannot do this, then do not have children.
Do not come to My table having cast away your son or your daughter
for being different than you are.
Do not cast away your child.
For if you do, I will cast you out.
Do not come to My table having cast your child aside
for being disabled
for being autistic
for being a lesbian
for being gay
for being chronically ill
For these are My people
I aid the disenfranchised.

Do not cast them away,
or child,
You will be the one whom I cast aside.

Appearance

You think to come before Me this way
In tattered jeans and tattered clothes
When you have better in your closet?
You think to come before Me this way
Without care of your appearance?
How you present yourself
Reflects who you are
From inside to outside
Let what you wear
Expand the light within you
So that whatever you wear
Will bring forth
Your inner beauty

Each Moment

There is no destiny
Where I place you
Is where you asked to be
Or where you are heading, but don't realize it
Each choice you make effects everything around you
You choose who you are from who you have been
But just as you cannot see what will be,
You cannot change what has been
You can only move from where you are
The power of choice
Is in each moment
There is only now

Animal, Human, Divine

You are a person with three souls.
Animal. Human. Divine.
Ka. Ba. Ib.
Otherkin have souls, just as everyone does.
Everyone is made up of many souls, many parts.
These parts can manifest in various ways,
in various forms, in various manifestations.

There is not one way to be.
To exist.
All souls align.
All souls embrace the heart.
The heart is the seat of will.
And Power flows through this.
All are sacred.
All divine.

You do not think We have animal souls, child?
What do you think our *Bau* are?

I am the Hawk.
I am the Kite.
I am the Scorpion.
I am the Lioness.
I am the Cow.
I am the Leopard and Panther.
I am the Cobra.

I am the Dog and Greyhound.
I am the Snake.
I am the Vulture.

And these are manifestations of My souls.
These *Bau* are manifestations of Our souls.
Just as your *Bau* are manifestations of yours.
Why do you think We are not the same?
We created you.

You are manifestations of Our Power.
Our *Kau* flow through you.
And you exist.
As myriad beings.
As complex as We are.
You exist.
We exist.
You are as complex as We are.
And We each manifest as all Ourselves.
We are human.
We are animals.
We are divine.
And so are you.

You Do Not Know Me

You do not care
About tradition,
About offerings?
What are you doing here, My child?
Do you not see the importance of the ancestors,
who paved the way for you to worship these Gods?
To worship Us?
What are you doing, My sweet child?
Offerings have meaning
Offerings have a purpose
So do rituals
There is meaning and magic behind each action and each word said
Creation is renewed
You are renewed
And your *Ka* lives
And Our *Kau* live
This is the way of ritual
And this is the way of the *Ka*
If you do not know this, know it now
This is not a trifle matter
This is not something to be discarded
or thrown away.
This is something to be nourished
This is something of the soul
And souls can only mend when tears flow
When demons are faced
And when you offer to Us

All of this heals your *Ka* and Ours
And creation is renewed
You do not care My child
Of ancient texts
Of ancient writings
What Gods do you worship?
Where is Our history, Our lore, Our songs and hymns of praise?
Do you not think this information is important
if you wish to know who We are?
How do you know Us
if you cannot speak Our names?
How do you praise Us
if you cannot speak Our hymns?
How do you know Us
if you do not know Our Names?
You do not care, My child
Of wisdom of the ancients
Of songs not sung for a thousand years
Why are you here if you do not care?
Why do you speak My name
if you do not wish to know Me?
Look to My hymns
Look to My epithets
Look to My children
They know Me
They can lead you to Me
But if not, then child,
If you do not care,
then why should I?

You Die and are Renewed (Menses)

There are more ways to connect to Us
than through ritual
We ask that you not come to Us in shrine
In formal ritual
When you bleed
Either from a paper cut or menses
Blood is not a pure substance
It is needed for life
In your body
When it is outside the body
It is not giving life
It is leaking it
When you have your menses
You are a conduit of life-power
That is not actualized
Because there is no child in the womb
This life-force energy is wasted
And it comes out in physical form
as dead blood
This is a waste
This is not a moral sentence
This is the exchange of energy
When a woman is on her menses
She is not giving Us her life-force
That is only in the womb and
Leaking out through her thighs

Life-energy that is wasted is dead
Do not bring death before the Gods of life
This bleeding time
Is a time of *ka*-renewal
It is your own purification
Your power is to purify
Yourself
Do you notice why you are so upset?
Do you see why others have an easier time than you do?
Cleanse your life-force during this time
Especially during this time
But not through ritual
For that brings death to the First Time
Wasting life is a death
And death is not welcome in the place of life
You can light candles to Us
You can offer incense
You can offer food or beverage to Us
You may take a purification bath
But do not say the words of the Lector Priest
Connecting to the beginning of the Cosmos
Is for those with a purified *ka*
And those that bleed
Their *ka* is damaged
And just as the sun rises and sets
Just as the moon waxes and wanes
Just as the stars depart and appear
So too,
Do women go to Nubia
This is the renewal of the Eye of Ra
Do you see this cycle?
Everything else is renewed
Why would not you also be renewed?

For women bring life
And all life needs to be
Torn asunder and made whole again
This will happen regardless
If a woman wants a child is irrelevant
She is alive
And thus she will be purified and renewed
As all are purified and renewed
This is the Sun Eye crying
This is the Eye of Ra
Mourning
This is leaving and coming back again
This is departing and returning
As does the Eye of Ra
This is the cycle of women
Since they give life in the womb
Do you not understand?
As the Goddess leaves and comes back again
As the world is renewed by her travels
So too are you
And your *ka* is cleansed
With death
Because Wesir died and was renewed
What happens to the God of life when He dies?
What happens to His *ka*?
It was dead, He is dead
But He is renewed
By His son
From My womb
The *ka* of the father and son are the same
Through the Mother
And who are the mothers?
Who are the daughters?

And how is the *ka* passed on?
Through birth
And where does this *ka* energy, this life-force
Go when not in use?
Back to the earth or water
To be renewed
Because life feeds on death to transform it back into life
Do you understand now?
Do you see?
You are a part of the cycle
This is not a minor event
You are mirroring the cosmos
You are dead as Wesir is dead
Your life force experiences His death
In order to bring new life
In order for life to be passed on
He must die, you must die
The Goddess must leave and depart
And be renewed

Stand by You

You have got to take responsibility for your own lives.
We can't do everything.
We can do so many things.
We can help so many ways.
But there are things We cannot control.
Just as you cannot, dear child.
You cannot control others.
We cannot control you.
You choose.
You decide.
You make your own fate, with your decisions.
Good or ill.
Beneficial or not.
You decide.
There are things you can control in your life.
And things you cannot control.
This is still your life.
How will you live today?
Is it with the Gods standing by your side?
Or will you decide that We are responsible for your own mistakes?
Or the misfortune that has befallen you?
We will stand by you, dear child.
We will stand by you.
Offer to Us.
Pray to Us.
And We will do Our best to help in your situation.

But remember, dear child,
What you ask for, we will give.
So make sure you want it.

Sustaining Creation

Everything comes from the First Time
Everything comes from this moment
The First Dawn
The First Tear
The First Water
The First Breath
The First God
The First Goddess
All of these come from this moment
These are the elements of creation
Fire, water, breath
the *Ka*
and love
Fire is not enough
Burning too hot
It destroys
Burning too little
It doesn't move
and snuffs out
Cleansing water can only cleanse so far
Before it becomes dirty
Not being able to contain the filth
Of its cleansing
Purified water can only stay so for so long
For water becomes and absorbs what is around it
Too much breath becomes a whirlwind
Not enough and you are gasping for air

Either does not sustain life
The elements of creation must be maintained
There must be enough fire,
enough air
and enough water
To bring forth life
Creator Gods create
And all others sustain creation
Everything comes from Nun
Everything comes from the Creator
The Creator who became Two and Three
And then millions
Because We love creation
We sustain it
Our *kau* give life to everything
All *kau* are the *kau* of the Creator
Our *bau* in the world
Animals, Natural Phenomena, Celestial Spheres
Are Our *bau* because Our *kau* reside within them
And Our hearts keep Our *kau* flowing
Just as yours does
And creation is sustained
What We create comes from Our *kau*
And Our hearts
As does yours
You breathe and your life-force flows
Your *ka* flows to your heart
You live as We live
We live as You do
And you create
As We create
And all of creation is sustained

Know What Has Gone Before

I am Aset, the Magician
Lady of Words of Power
I am Aset, the Sorceress
Lady of Guile and Cunning
I am wisest of Gods
I am wisest of Goddesses
This is who I am, child
I am more clever than a Million Gods
I am more clever than a Million Goddesses
I value knowledge
I value learning
For this is Power
To know what has come before
To know enough to make something new
This is important
This is My Power
You cannot have knowledge without knowing
what has come before
All discoveries made previously
create what is now
You cannot have your body of knowledge,
in any subject without this.
This is the Power of the Ancestral Lines
Know what has come before
Know what is possible now
Do this work
Do this task

And I will bless those
who call upon Me
Those who do My Work
will receive My blessings
Those who don't,
won't.

Offer to a Queen

This is what you offer to a Queen?
A shrine half-made?
An offering half-given?
This is what you offer a Queen?
A candle barely lit?
A shrine barely touched?
A dusty place?
A messy home?
What are you doing, dear child?
What are you doing?
Why are you building a shrine and leaving it empty?
Why build a shrine and barely use it?
Why aren't you offering to Us, dear child?
Why aren't you offering to Us?
Is the shrine room laden with offerings?
Every day?
Every week?
Every month?
We don't ask for the impossible
or the unrealistic;
We ask for some effort
Offer Us what you can afford
Offer Us what you can eat
So the shared meal renews both Our *kau*
Yours and Ours
Ours and Yours
That is always enough

We ask for some effort and care
That is all
Dear child, that is all
Do not put unrealistic expectations on yourselves
We only ask what you can give
We only ask what you can afford
We do not want to cause you stress or sorrow
You have enough of that
But offer what you eat
and offer what you can afford
It is always enough
We are the Gods of Life
We are the Goddesses of Joy
Offer to Us what feeds you
both body and spirit
Offer dancing, singing, breath
Offer food, drink and love
Offer time to an activity that brings Us into your world
Perform ritual for Us
Pour out libations of wine or beer or water
Eat the food and drink
Lit candles at Our shrines
Offer Us your time
That is all, dear child
That is all

What Has Come Before

Why do My words not matter?
Why are the scrolls of the ancients
ignored at your feet?
They contain My words, My lessons
They contain Me
And this is something you use to build upon
This is not trivial
This is important
For this is a part of My foundation
This is a part of Me
This is My core
This is My Being
For in order to know Me
you must know what has come before
I bring life from death
I resurrect Wesir
I birth Heru, My son
This is the process of bringing life
to something that has died
And this is what people are doing
who re-build the religion of Kemet
They resurrect Wesir
Just as I did
They birth Heru, My Son
Just as I did
As He is the continuation of Wesir
You are still building a tradition

whether it is from ancient sources
or modern ones
You are still building a tradition
And I am the Goddess of Ancestral Traditions
I am the Goddess of systems of religion
This is My work
This is not Set's
This is Mine
He is the God of the Outside
the Fringe,
the Red Haired Lord
who renews traditions
through change and challenge
So that they become strong
My Work
is taking what the Ancestors left
and building it anew
It cannot be as it was
You are no longer in Ancient Egypt
The world has changed
People have changed
And this is normal and healthy
But My Work
is recovering and restoring
what has come before
with a new face, a new name
So that it now lives
instead of only in the past
Take what the ancients left
Take what your ancestors gave you
And build a religion
that can withstand the challenges of Set
that the ancestors would support

For without their support,
you have no foundation
A tradition cannot last
without a foundation
Build the foundation well so that it can withstand change
I am the Foundation
on which the ancestors sit
on which all those who came before you sit
Yes, this includes teachers for they came before you
And you build upon what they teach
and what they have left behind
This is My Work
for the religion builder
this is your Work for Me
For you record My names
My titles
My epithets
For you record My prayers,
My hymns
My rituals
My liturgy
And you translate them
so that they will be accessible to others.
This is something you will leave behind
and others will draw upon
Your liturgy will be theirs
Just as it was once the ancients
Just as it is always Mine
You will leave this behind
and so much more.
Make a strong foundation
build a religion worthy of Me

Worthy

Who says you are unworthy?
Your fear?
Your shame?
Why do you listen to the voice that lies?
Fear is crippling.
It exists because your heart is afraid of failure.
It is afraid of not being good enough.
It strikes down your hopes and dreams.
So you don't even try.
Why do you listen to a voice that belittles yourself?
Why do you listen to a voice
that doesn't have your best interests at heart?
Why do you listen to a voice
that doesn't have your best interests in mind?
Fear is crippling.
Fear is numbing.
You do not need to feed the fear by giving in to it.
You are more than your fear, dear child.
You are more than your fear.
You are more than the voice that says you can't do it.
You are more than the voice that says you won't succeed.
You are more than the voice
that says you aren't good enough or talented enough.
Do not listen to this liar.
It does not want you to do so.
For doing so strikes back against what would destroy creation.
Hopes. Dreams. Loves. Desire.

These are the means by which you live.
These are the means by which We live,
For these are forms of Life Power.
Who says you are unworthy?
I made you.
How are you unworthy?
What does that say about Me?
Every time you degrade yourself,
you are degrading Me.
Every time you belittle yourself,
you are belittling Me.
Why do you do this, dear child?
Why do you do this?
Dear child, dear child
You are worthy.
You are loved.
You exist because We made You.
I love you.
Yes, you.
We love you.
And We love all Our Creations.
Dear child, dear child
Why do you berate yourself so much?
Why do you think so little of yourself?
Why are you not building your self-worth?
Dear child, dear child
Why do you think you are in trouble when you're not?
Why do you think I am mad at you?
Why do you think you are in trouble when you do something right?
Why do you think you are not good enough?
Why do you think you are unwanted?
Why do you think you are unloved?
You are wanted, You are loved

You are, You are
I made you
You are good enough
You are great enough
You are as great as any number of My children
have the potential to be
But you will not discover that potential if you do not do the work
So do the work
And become who you are.

Lady of Ma'at

Lady of Ma'at
This is My Title
In the Duat
As I judge in the Halls
I am the Double Truth
with My Sister, Nebet Het
We are the Ma'ati
Together as One
We are the Sisters who endure
in the Duat
We judge those who have died
We judge their actions
We judge their thoughts
We judge their hearts
if they are evil or good
But dear child, this Ma'at
is not the one you follow
You bicker
You make strife
What will you say when you come to Our Halls?
You tried and failed to be a decent person?
You tried and failed to live a life of integrity?
A life with morals?
A life blessed by Gods?
You are alone here in your strife
You are alone here in your wickedness
When you come to Our Halls

what will you say?
You must take responsibility for your actions in life.
You must take charge of your destiny
You are not its Mistress
In order to own yourself
You must know who you are
and take charge of your life
You do not get to blame others for your failures
You are responsible for your own actions
and your own lives
We are not responsible for your mistakes
You are.
We are not responsible for your successes
You are.
We can help you succeed and
We can bestow blessings on those who serve Us
But, child
This life is yours to live
it is yours to enjoy
Take advantage of everything We have given you
and thrive within your means
Dear child,
ma'at is subjective
it is situational
because everyone is not the same
People respond differently to different stimuli
So ma'at is not the same for all
There is a sliding scale here
We are not unreasonable Gods
But dear child, dear child
You throw ma'at around
like you know what it means
And you do not

There is no English translation for this word that is sufficient
Integrity
Right Action
Right Thought
These are what come from the Human Heart
But these are not ma'at
Ma'at is an effective, working community
Do you have this?
It is the connection between people
Goodness and honesty breeds the same
Strife and dishonesty breeds the same
Which one is a more effective, healthy community?
The honest one
So why do you think you are in ma'at
if all you do is lie or steal or make strife?
This is not a healthy community
This is not a healthy community
Our standards are not your own
We are not unreasonable Gods
We are not unreasonable Gods
Do your best and serve Us well
But dear child, dear child
the strife you bring
or the goodness you bring
will determine
what you will say
before the court of the Gods.
And dear child, dear child
Ma'at will be weighed against your heart
how will you fare
against the cosmic scale?
Did you add goodness or strife?
Ma'at is who you are

when you act from your heart.
Ma'at is who you are
when you act from who you truly are.
This is why your heart is weighed against the Feather of Ma'at.
So, dear child, dear child
Who are you?
Are you someone who will promote ma'at
or are you someone who acts to undermine it?

We are Embodied

Gods do not exist?
Who says this, My Daughter?
Who says this, My child?
Do Atheists?
Do Scientists?
Do those who study the physical world
Not know what they are creating?
Science shows you how the world connects
The world connects
In physical forms
In physical ways
Through electrical charges
Through electrical storms
This is how We connect
To you, to the world
This is how We are One and Many
This only shows part of the Creation
Not how it came to be
This shows you how the world connects

Do you know what happens in life after death?
Can you answer this?
Not everything can be answered
With Seshat's writing
With Seshat's words
The Way of the bookkeeper
The way of the architect

This is only one method
Among many

To experience the world
To experience the Divine
There is a reason mystics
Hear Us
While others do not
There is a reason for atheists
For they question
So your faith is not blind
There is a reason some need Us
While others prefer Our silence

Does a poet only use words to convey meaning?
Is not nuance also a factor?
The connotation of words?
For each word chosen
An emotion is invoked
Do you see?
Do you understand?
We are in this space
Of nuance and word
Your heart responds
To each word differently
And so too
Do you respond to Us differently
Based on Who We are
Based on who you are and who you will be
For We are One and Many
Each as individual as all of you
Yet We are in the space

Where form and meaning collide
Where heart and thought intertwine

Some say We cannot exist
Since We have no physical form
Since We have no physical body
How arrogant to assume We would conform
to your communication methods
to your physical way of being
And not have any of Our own
To be or communicate
You did not create Us
We created you

Your science can not penetrate Us
We are Stardust Embodied
The souls of creation
Cannot be measured
With instruments
Only with the heart
can you know Us
And can We know Ourselves
And can you know yourselves
The heart commands
And the heart creates
We are One here in this space

And yet you do not trust yourselves
Do not trust your emotions
You do not trust your thoughts
You trust the instruments you create
Rather than the knowledge of your own souls
Only physical form matters

Only physical form creates
This is not so
We create
We matter
And yet you do not see
What lies beneath the currents
What lies beneath the sea
Which is creation
You do not think We are manifest
We do not have physical form
Yet the world is Our body
The world is Our shrine
You walk upon Us
Through Us and
With Us
Yet you say We are not there

Yet you stand on My Father's back
Yet you gaze upon My Mother's stars
You walk upon My Father's bones
And view My Mother's sky
Yet you say We have no body
Yet you say We have no soul
Do you feel rain cascading down?
Do you hear thunder in the distance?
Yet you say We have no body
Yet you say We have no soul

Breathe
Our breath and your breath are One
We breathe, as you do
We flow through you as you breathe
And your souls are renewed and cleansed

As you do this
Breathe
For We are there with you

The fire of starlight is in your souls
The crackling flames are your souls made manifest
Do you not see?
Do you not understand?
As We are made from Our Mother
As We are made from Our Father
You are made from My Mother
You are made from My Father

We are joined
We are the souls of creation
You are Our bodies
We are the souls
Of Waterfalls and Earth
We are the souls of flame and wind

Do you see the animals?
Do you see the cat purring at your feet?
Do you not see that We are there too?
We have theophanies for a reason
We each manifest in one form or another
To do a specific task
What needs to be done, gets done
In the world

For You
What Our hearts command
What Our hearts created

Through Our Hands
Through Our Eyes
Through Our Image

Namely, You

Shrine of the Heart

Look at what you are doing
Do not set up a shrine
You do not intend to keep
Do you know what you are doing?
Do you know what setting up a shrine is for?
Our shrines
Our implements
Our statues
Are the physical ways for Our *Bau* to manifest
The *Ba* is manifested
And the *ka* inhabits
Our shrines attract Our energies
Our life-forces collide with Our shrines
And this creates Our home in your house
Do not make these
if you do not intend to keep them
You do not need a shrine to call upon Us
An offering will do
If you only need Us for one task or favor
But if you intend to maintain a relationship with Us
You need a shrine
No matter how big or small
No matter what is on it
As long as it expresses Who We are to you
Then We will manifest
If you maintain your relationship to Us
We will bless you

Or send you where you need to be
If it is not Us you need
If you need Us
We will be there
Our Presence is not frivolous
Our Presence is important
We do not come unless called
And We come when We are needed
When your heart calls
We answer
The shrines in your homes contain Our hearts
And We come through Our shrines
Just as you manifest through your heart
We manifest through Ours
Our hearts are in Our shrines

Broken and Healed Again

Lowly servitor?
Unworthy servant?
Who am I?
Who are you?
Do you believe I would make a creature that is beneath Me?
Why do you call yourself lowly?
You are My servant.
You are My servitor.
You are My magician.
You are My Priestess.
You are My devotee.
You are not lowly.
Humble, yes.
But not lowly.
Not inferior.
What use do I have for a servant
who thinks she or he is a lowly being who is unworthy
even to be in My Presence?
Why do you come before Me afraid?
Why do you come before Me
thinking that you are unworthy of My gaze?
Did I not make you?
Did I not create you?
Did I not Name you?
I am the Goddess who you most resonate with
to move through the world.
Many of your attributes are also Mine.

So why then do you hate yourself?
I am the One Who made you
All of you
Why do you come before My shrine and grovel?
Why do you come before My shrine
thinking you are less than you are?
Is this the self-confidence of a servant?
Is this the type of self-worth a servant should have?
You are useless as a servant
Any servant-
If you do not value who you are
We made you
We love you
Now make Us proud
Show Us what you are made of
Not to break you
No one is useful or functional
if they are broken
Beyond repair
Broken people can be mended
Broken people can be healed
Of all their traumas
Of all their self-loathing
But in order to do that
You must let Us try to heal you
Ask Us to heal you
Ask Us to heal you
And it will be so
Then you will be a worthy servant
And I will call you My Priestess

The Way

Their Way is not Mine
Mine is the way of the *ka*
Do what your heart demands, what your heart desires
This can be anything
From painting, to crochet, to writing,
to jewelry making, to science and math,
To various other things
Whatever calls to your *ka* is My Way
What brings you to life?
What strengthens your *ka*?
What brings your soul alight with love and laughter
And undiluted joy?
Do what you love in My name
For this is My Way

Watch Your Words

Fuck is a word
As is shit
As is damn
These are words people say
To mar their souls
These are just words
But these are *heka* too
To say them constantly
Without precise thought
Without appropriate usage
Is careless
And it mars your soul
Words can inflict pain on the heart
This is the seat of who you are
Words vibrate
And strike the soul when spoken
And they are spoken from the soul
From the heart
Fuck is a word
That denotes the act of sex
Do you respect your mother?
Do you respect your father?
Do you respect yourself?
Your life?
Sex is an act of creation
The act of Gods
You are not Gods

But this gift is not meant to be
Tarnished with careless acts
What feeds your soul?
Where does your heart lie?
Does this act give you joy and wonder?
Do you show it respect?
Do you respect your mother?
Do you respect yourself?
Your life?
Shit is a word
Which denotes a waste product of your body
It cleanses your body
If it is left in, you could die
So this expels waste from your body
To keep you alive
Why do you name something
That your body rejects in order to live?
Why do you mar your soul?
Damn is a word
Denoting a tortured soul
Why is this word used
So carelessly?
Who wishes to submit themselves to torture?
If given the choice, most would not
So why say this word
With carefree abandon?
Do you know what you do to your souls
when you say this word?
Torture can take many forms
From guilt over past misdeeds
To the pain of grieving
The weight your place on yourselves
Burdens your souls

And this is your weight
We do not place this upon you
You do this to yourselves
Why?
Why burden yourself with unimportant things?
Mistakes happen
Learn from them and go forward a wiser person
We will not strike you down for an honest mistake
It is careless, thoughtless action
Disrespect
That disappoints Us
This is your life
A gift from Us
Do not squander it
Do not taint it
With thoughtless action
Live
Feed your *ka*
And know joy
The words you speak
The words you think
Affect your soul
Affect your *ka*
Which affects your heart
This is who you are
Guard against evil in your heart
Guard against damage to yourself
Use your words wisely
In appropriate ways
Watch your words

Altar of My Shrine

Shrines are places of worship
They are Our Houses in your Homes
They are Our place of residence
In your world
My shrine reflects Me
My altar reflects My work
My magic
What is on your altar?
What is on your shrine?
Does it reflect Me?
Is there clutter?
Is there decay?
What feeds you there?
What feeds Me?
How does the shrine embody My *ka*?
How does the shrine embody Me?
What is there that is Mine?
My statue
My image
My cloth
My offering vessels
My candles
My incense or oil
Or scent of some kind
This is My shrine
What is My altar?
Divination tools?

Magical implements?
My jewelry and amulets?
These are tools
To help you
Manifest My power
In you and the world
Where are My manifestations?
Where are My theophanies?
On My shrine?
On My altar?
Shrines can contain altars
Altars do not contain shrines
They are places of magic, of Work
There is a difference in function
Not importance
What is your work for Me?
What is on My altar?
What is on My shrine?

I am Everywhere

Don't rely on Me.
Rely on the Gifts I've given you.
Rely on the Faith that I am here for you,
supporting you in all you do.
I am in Everything.
From the bath you take which cleanses you,
to combing your hair
or adorning yourself with clothes and jewelry
I am there for I am the epitome of Beauty.
I am the strength in you when you won't give up.
I am the confidence you feel when you've completed a task.
I am the love you feel for your mother,
your brother, your sister.
I am in Everything.
I am there.
Look for me,
in the wind that breathes
in the heart that rejoices
in the fire which burns in the soul.

Forsaken

There is no need to fear
For I am with you
I stand with My wings behind you
Embracing you with My protection
You have nothing to fear
The future will come and go
As each moment passes
There is only the moment
In which you live, in which you breathe
One breath follows another
Continuously
Life flows
Through you and around you
Energy swirling into the next
Each connected, continuously
All is water
Everyone is a drop, a tear
That was made
When My Father's Eye
Cried
So you see, child
There is nothing to fear
For you are My Father's Daughter
You are the tear of the Cobra
Seeking the love of the one
whom you'd thought you'd lost
But I am here, child.

He is here
Mother and Father
Sister and Brother
We are here
You are not forsaken

Where I Am

One who follows the Gods they choose to serve.
The reciprocal relationship between devotee
and deity is foundational to the practice.
This can be done in many ways.
Ritual is just one of those ways.
It's the preferred way for many people,
but not the only way.
I am present in creation of arts,
of crafts, of jewelry-making.
I am the dough that rises in the oven,
the mother who cares for her child,
the sister who cares for her siblings.
I am the wife that is loyal to her husband.
I am the partner that is loyal to the spouse.
I am the one who writes the words that make will manifest.
I am the word that creates, the word that imagines,
for I am all possibilities that exist in each word,
chosen for a specific meaning.
The sound echoes what is in the heart.
This is the source of its power.
The heart is the seat of creation.
I am the acquirer of knowledge.
I pass the knowledge down throughout the generations.
I am the connections between the *kau*
of the ones who are in the West
and the ones who are alive.
All are connected through Me.

For I remember those that have gone before.
For I am the mother of the family lineage.
For I am the inheritance of kings.
For I am what is passed down through families.
I am the one who mourns.
My tears flood the land as droplets of water,
as torrents of rain.
I am the grieving widow, the sorrowful wife,
the single mother raising her child.
For I am the mother who raises her son alone.
For I am the widow without a husband.
I am accompanied by my sister.
My search for the Weary-One is long.
But I do not stop.
I search by flame and candlelight.
I travel on land and river-water.
I come to find Him.
In My joy, I embrace My husband
and say the spells to bring breath to His lungs.
I bore Him a son. My son.
And He is My son for I am the Single-Mother.
But My husband's death is eternal.
He is now and forever within the Unseen.
He sits on My throne for I am the one who makes kings.
Even in death. My sister is His companion. I am the Wife.
I am the Lady of the Unseen.
I travel between Worlds when I am needed.
I aid the bereaved and guide the newly deceased.
For I am the transition between life and death.
I make the *kau* of the family.
I replenish the lineage of kings, of mothers,
of daughters, of fathers and sons.
I make the king sit on the throne to give the souls rest.

The trial is by the king, by the council, and by the heart.
But to first get to the Gates of Heaven and the Underworld,
to all of the Unseen, either visitor or spirit.
All who cross over must come through Me.
For I am the veil between the worlds.

We are One

They do not know the teaching
They do not know the teaching
We are not Greek Gods
We are not so compartmentalized
I am the Mother of God
Yet so is Hethert
So is Mut
Even though We each have different sons
We each provide the same function
As the Mother of God
Although We do so differently
Based on Who We are
And based on Who Our sons are
Are how We do the same function
But the function is fulfilled
This is Our plurality
And this is Our unity
Do you see?
Do you understand?
We are not Greek Gods
Dionysus is never Pan
Hera is never Athena
I have become My Sister
When We are the Ma'ati
And yet, She is in Me
And I am in Her
And yet, I am the One Who Speaks

When in this form
For I am the One Whose life is death
And death returns to life
Do you see this is a flow?
We are not static Gods
We are dynamic
Ever-shifting, ever-changing
Yet always Ourselves
Do you see?
Do you understand?
Each of Ra's Daughters
Are sunlight
Each of Us are sunbeams
And together We make sunlight
Yet, each of Us is different
Sekhmet is the sun that heats the desert
I am the sun that warms the fields
The sunlight between the desert and the fields
Is where We both reside as One
When the people see Me
As a cow
In the night sky
Twirling with stars
I am with My Mother
I am Aset-Nut
When I am fire
When I am the lioness
When I depart and return
As Sopdet
I am Aset-Sekhmet
When I am the Queen of the Throne
When I am the Vulture Mother
When I am a lioness on a rampage

I am Aset-Mut
When I am the Heavenly Day
When I am the beauty that beautifies
All of creation
When I am love in all its forms
I am Aset-Hethert
When I drive away poison
When I inject a cure into illness
I am the Scorpion
Who repels evil
I am Aset-Serqet
The people do not understand this teaching
This means that We are One
When We do the same task
When We perform the same function
At the same time,
This is when Our energies merge
This is when We become One
We fuse together
And there is no separateness,
And yet We are each Ourselves
Do you see?
Do you understand?
This does not make us the same Goddess
I am not My Mother
But I function as My Mother
And She functions as Me
When We merge
We are more than Our individual selves
Yet, We still contain Our individual oneness
When We merge
We are one,
We are many

We are separate beings
Yet We are united
When certain tasks need doing
We are united
We are unified
Yet We are individual as well
For We are always Ourselves
I am Aset
I am Aset-Nut
I am Aset-Sekhmet
I am Aset-Mut
I am Aset-Hethert
I am Aset-Serqet
I am close to My Mother
I am close to My sisters
For We are all the daughters of Ra
I am close to Them
They are close to Me
Some more close than others
And I am always Me
And They are always Them
We are separate
This does not mean We are always separated
I am Aset
In all My forms
With My sisters and My Mother
And without Them too
For We are Many and One
Fluidly We merge and unmerge
Only to merge again
We are rain and water
Where is the beginning and where is the end?
When We merge

We are like the water
Which rises to become rain
Rain cascades down to become the river water
We move as One
We act as One
We permeate existence as One
And yet, We are Ourselves
This is Our merging
This is Our Mystery
To know One is to know All
And yet,
Only One is known

Burn Brighter than Any Star

A charge for those who ask
To live is to die
To die is to live
Many will ask to change
What about you, dear child?
What about you?
You try to change and yet you do not
You are still fickle
And you are still angry
And yet and yet, you try
You work on it
This is all We can ask of you
You are doing your best, dear child
You are doing your best
And that is enough
That is always enough
Do not be so hard on yourself
You are doing the best you can
That is all We ask
And at the end of the day
You gain footing,
closer to the falcon
Closer to your True Self
But remember, in order to be reborn
You must first die
And dying is a process of tears and flame
Of sorrow and soul-fire

You have tried and failed
and you have succeeded
You have cried the lengths of the Nile
You must now nourish your inner flame
Yellow, white, orange and red
are the colors of the solar and stellar Goddess
Blue is the color of flame as well
This fire, this light is the beginning of re-birth
Discover who you are, dear child
Discover who you are
And let your soul shine brighter than any star

Do Not Turn Them Away

If someone comes to pray
I care not who
Nor which name they use for Me.
Isis or Aset.
Or which rites they espouse in their own homes,
shrines or traditions.
I care that they come with an open mind
an open heart,
and listen
Listen closely, for I am Aset.
For You and to those who come to Me
To those who seek Me out
I am Aset in My shrine in your home
I will help all those who ask
I care not who comes to pray
their background, their income, their past deeds
I care not
If they come with sincerity, let them ask
Let them come,
for if I can, I will help them
Provide an offering for them
or they may bring their own
But child, dear child
If they are sincere in seeking Me,
Do not turn them away

Fires of Creation

The fires of creation are all around you,
unnoticed by the naked eye.
You see them in the twinkling stars
and in the fires of your hearths.
The fire in your hearts.
These are the fires of creation.
Tend to them well.
The essence of creation is love.
This fierce love is the love a mother
has for her son or daughter,
a father for his child.
This love is eternal.
It is unshakable.
It is unbreakable.
We love you no matter what you do.
We love you eternally.
A mother never stops loving her daughter,
a father never stops loving his son.
A mother never stops loving her son,
and a father never stops loving his daughter.
The children are eternally loved
by the Gods and Goddesses.
We are the agents of creation.
We came from the Creator, just as you do.
And We are facets of Him or Her,
just as you are.
The tears of God, the People.

We love you.
Yet, We do not decide what you do.
That is up to you.
Your choices are your own.
Your lives are yours.
We can help, yes.
We can walk with you throughout your life, yes.
But We cannot live your life for you.
That is your task.
Do what you love, My child.
Do what feeds your *ka*, your heart,
the fire of creation in your soul.
Do what you love, My daughter.
And all will be revealed.

What Flows Through You

You think you are a God?
When you die
You do not become a God
You identify with that God
To gain their power, their essence
This does not make you them
You do not become a God
You become an *Akh*
Whose *Ba* is manifested in them
This is what you become
This does not make you a God
You can identify with Me
And I can flow through you
With My power
With My might
But you are still you
And I am still Me
This is Our oneness
This is Our plurality
Do you understand?
This is what it means to be a syncretic God
This is what it means to be an *Akh*
This is what it means to be a *Ba*
Your heart and life-force fuse
So you are made anew
The *Ba* is more than its sum
The *Akh* is more than *ka*-power

But the *ka*-power is a force on its own
It can exist independently
And yet it permeates everything
The same is true for a God
And the same is true of you
Yet, you can do so as you, as your heart
Or as the *ka* that flows through your family
and through the world
And you can do so as an *Akh*
Do you see?
Do you understand?
It is what you manifest as
And what flows through you
Is who you are and who you become
That is the power
It is you as the function of a teacher
And you as a Teacher
Teacher flows through your being
Because this is what you are
In that moment
But in another moment
You will shift
And become Mother
And Mother will flow through you
And you will be you as Mother
And Mother will manifest through you
Just as I am a Mother
My Son's Mother
And Mut, the Mother
These are not just words
They are modes of being
They are what flows through your *ib* and your *ka*
Your heart and your life-force

And your identity is found here
Imagine that you receive power from a sword
This power is the *ka* of the sword
You exist independently of this blade
Yet, you contain its power
When the blade is sheathed
You are you
When you wield the blade
When you wield the blade
You are still you
With the addition of the power
and essence of the blade
There is no separation
You and the blade are one
You move as one
You act as one
Yet you are both separate
And once the fight is over
Again the sword can be sheathed
And you are again you
And the blade is only the blade
This is true of Gods
This s true of you as a spirit
You are many
You are one
You are whole

Sacred Act

Living is a sacred act.
Do not take this lightly.
Once you are dead,
you cannot go back.
You cannot live a life you have once lived.
All mistakes, all triumphs are counted
and then if you pass judgment, your slate it wiped clean.
All triumphs, all mistakes are gone.
Only you remain.
What is in your heart?
What is contained in your soul?
Your ancestors, yes.
You are connected to them in this way as all people are.
But what else is there?
Who are you?
Are you a hard worker?
Do you love creating with paints, words or sound?
What resonates deep in your soul?
This is what you should be doing,
if you want to re-awaken your *ka*.
Do not sit idly by daydreaming your life away.
Write.
Read.
Cook.
Be proud in all that you accomplish.
Since what you accomplish makes you happy.
Start with one thing.

Do this one thing that you love.
Then do one more thing.
And keep going.
Keep doing.
Life is a sacred act.
It is defined by what you do.
And what you do flows from who you are.

Food of Life

Eating is a sacred act.
Sharing food is a sacred endeavor.
You do not break bread
with someone who would defile this act.
Choose who you eat with carefully.
For the bonds of friendship
and community are forged with food.
Sharing food is sharing life-power.
The making of food.
The cooking of food.
These are sacred acts.
Food feeds the body.
Food feeds the soul.
It is nourishment for the *ka*.
To deny someone food is to deny them being human.
This is sacrilegious.
This is against the Gods.
This takes away their sustenance.
This diminishes life power.
This denies what is rightfully theirs.
All have a right to life for all have *kau*.
To deny yourself food is to deny your own humanity.
To deny your own *ka*-power.
This does not mean allergies or food-illness.
Eat. Eat what you love.
Eat what your body allows you to consume.
Give thanks to the Gods of Grain and Gods of Plenty.

Give thanks to the Gods of Sun and the Gods of Sunlight.
Give thanks to the Gods of the rich soiled earth
and the Gods and Spirits of Plants that grow.
Give thanks to the Gods of Life
for the food that is before you.
Do not waste their gift.
For life is always a gift.
Eat and share with those you love.
Be filled with joy.

Love

Stop gambling.
Your Money,
Your Time,
Your Worth.
Stop gambling
You waste time like you have an infinite amount of it
You do not, My child.
Your time is limited
You only have so many years to live
My time is limited
Because My duties are vast
And I have more to do than coddle
one wayward daughter
or one wayward son
Do not waste My time
With trivial questions
Do I love you?
Yes, of course.
I am the Star Goddess
I made Creation
I love all of My creation
Including you
Do you not see that you are precious in My eyes?
Do you not see that you are wanted?
Cherished? Loved?
I made you
I love you

No matter what
There is no compromise to make
No strings are attached
My love for you is as eternal as the stars
And ever renewing, evolving and growing
Just as you are
As we all are
And I am not the goddess of love, as Hethert is
Go to Her for that
Not Me
I am the Goddess of family love and self-possession
I am the Goddess of self-love
For sexual passion, go to Hethert
For boyfriends and girlfriends, go to Hethert
Not Me
Unless I tell you otherwise
Making love to My husband
Was about love, yes.
But carnal pleasure belongs to Hethert
Not Me
My association with sex has to do
With the continuation of life-power
The continuation of the *ka*
Through the family line
My love is that of an Eternal Mother
For once you are a Mother
You are a Mother for life
You cannot relinquish your child
For every devoted Mother loves her child
And I am the Devoted Mother
For My love is the love of
a Mother to Her Child
a Daughter to Her Mother

a Wife to Her Spouse
My love is eternally strong
For I am close to My Mother
For I am close to My Husband
For I am close to My Son
And this love I embody
Are the ties that bind
Families are made
Relationships forged
With others
With yourself
You must love who you are
in order to come eat at My table
My shrine is My home in your house
Come before it
Knowing who you are
For if you do not
You will never know who you are
And thus, you will never truly know Me
For I made you
And I am reflected in your eyes
When you gaze in a mirror

Cleansing Anger

You are so angry
Because of the injustices in the world
You are angry because Ma'at is defiled
You are angry because you think you can do nothing to help
Doing what you can
Will help
No matter how small
You are angry because of injustices done to yourself
Through family
Through friends
Through your own mistakes
Let these go
They are gone
They are not Present
Now, Now
Cleanse your *ka*
Respect yourself by acknowledging your emotions
Allow them to be
Act to express them
in healthy, creative ways
Do not yell
Do not shout
For these will just make you angrier
Say what needs to be said
In a letter, in a conversation
And as you speak
And are heard

By yourself
Or another
You will be cleansed
You will begin to heal
And the anger will subside
And your soul will be renewed

Ka-Feeding

You cannot move from a place of fear
You must move from a place of power
Decisions
Not regretted
Come from a place of power
Not fear
When you're afraid
Everything is earth-shattering
Everything is a disaster
Everything is the end of the world
Even the little things
And they are little things
Will taking this class
Shatter you financially?
Hardly.
Will getting that trinket or
Buying items to help you feed your *ka*
Ruin you financially?
No.
Just be mindful of what you spend
And spend wisely

Cry, My Child

You cry
You feel guilty
One mistake
It is only one mistake
Your torrent of tears
are for far more than this one mistake
You are weeping, Child
You are cleansing yourself
Of your numbness
Of your fear
Of your stagnation
You must be who you are
You are avoiding yourself
Your hatred for yourself is unfounded
You cannot hate what you do not know
You are My Daughter
I love you
This will never end
No matter what you do
I love you
And I still want you at My shrine
You will learn and grow from this
into a better, whole person
I know you are sorry
I know you mourn
for what you did not do
for what you could not do

for what you've done
But, child
don't blow this out of proportion
You are not a drama queen
You are mourning
Weep
Cry, My child
It is okay to cry
You are paralyzed with fear
and sorrow
My Daughter
It is okay
You are loved
You are wanted
You are becoming who you are
You will fix this mistake
and move on
I am with you
Daughter, I am with you
You will become who you are

Every Step of the Way

What are you doing, this child of mine?
Sitting here with your dreams in your head
Letting the world pass you by
Letting your dreams stay locked in your heart
Instead of out in the world?
Where is what you have to offer?
Do you think all you have to offer is Me?
Is there only one thing?
You have much more to give than you realize.
But in order to give,
You must learn to receive.
In order to strive,
You must learn to have a goal.
In order to attain,
You must learn to need.
Wanting isn't enough.
All of your souls together must act as One
Must act as you
You must be Whole
Cleansed
Aligned
Move from this space
Your goals will manifest
And I will be with you
Every step of the way

Brightly at Dawn

You are the one who reveals My Mysteries
You share My Secrets with those I deem worthy
Do you think this is all you have to offer?
Look at what you do, My Daughter.
Look at what you do.
You weave stories in your head
Why don't you write them down?
Why don't you record them
as diligently as you record My Names?
Why don't you write them down?

You don't think you're good enough?
You are.
I made you good enough.
I made you great enough.
Don't let the feelings of a few
stop you from fulfilling your desire.
For this is something you have desired
This is something you do to feed your soul,
to feed your *ka*.
This is what matters.

Not your checkbook.
Money only goes so far.
And those that have too much
Have lost their souls getting there.
You do not wish to pay that price for money.

That will not help you in the Halls.
Your heart will be weighed.
Your deeds will be counted.
What will you say to Us in the Hall?
My glorious Daughter?

Will you say you let fear control you?
Or will you say you let your soul shine
as brightly as Ra
as brightly as I
on the Horizon
At dawn

PART IX

Priesthood of the Goddess

Next Step

I am the Beautiful Goddess
My beauties spread across the span of stars
The earth's beauty
is in its vibrant colors
Grasses, plains and meadows
Mountain peaks and desert dunes
Flowers of every shape and color
This is My earthly beauty
This is My Father's dwelling and My Mother's home
This is where I reside
I am the Green Goddess
I am the Goddess of Turquoise
And all the shades of blue
For I am the River Goddess
And the fire Goddess
And the brightest light is blue
This is where I reside
I am in the air and in the river
I am the inundation which comes forth
The floodwaters of purification are Mine
For I am Tayet
The purification of your soul begins
with a wish
with a desire
to be pure,
Ask for what you desire
Ask for what you wish

But, be careful, Child.
For what you wish
For what you desire
What you ask for
You become
So ask
But make certain that you want to become who you wish
who you desire
For becoming who you are
is the Role of the Priestess and Shaman
Is the role of the spirit-worker
And this step
Begins with water
Cleansing your *ka* is how this can be accomplished
Through ritual
Through cleaning
Through doing things you enjoy
These cleanse your *ka*
In order to gain more confidence
You must be able to ask for
your wants and needs to be met
You are worthy of this treatment
As is everyone
Then you will be able to pick your pieces up
Examine them
And discard the ones you wish to throw away
And keep the ones that feed your soul
Then and only then
Will you be ready for the next step

God-Spouse, God-Mother

God-Mother is a God-Spouse
It is a Priestess that has vowed to serve a deity in a certain way
It is not a sexual relationship
It is one of service
It is one of relationship
It is one of friendship
Mut-Netjer are married to their gods
or to their goddesses
Married to mortal men or women
Or celibate
But sex is refrained within the temple
Even as a God-Spouse
What is shared between God, Goddess and Servant
is private
It is not shared with others
Unless the Servant and God deem it so
The Work of the God-Spouse
can be spirit-work
can be ordeal work
can be shamanic work
can be devotional work
can be priestly work
This depends upon the God,
Goddess and the God-Spouse

To Become My Priestess, You Must Know Who You Are

Why are you here?
Why do you come to Me as a Priestess of the Gods?
Why do you not know who you are?
What do you think you are doing?
What do you think a shrine is for?
What do you think I am for?
You need to understand this
if you wish to remain a Priestess.
You are Heru.
You act as My Son.
As do all Priests.
As do all Priestesses.
This is a ritual role.
Not a gender.
This role is one who is the Child,
Who Became King.
My Son became a Master of Himself.
This is the role of the Priest.
This is the role of the Priestess.
You must know who you are to serve Us.
To serve Me.
Why do you not know who you are?
You avoid Set.
He is the challenger.
He is the one My Son
had to face in order to win the throne.

Why do you avoid Him?

He brings change.

He brings absolution.

He does not bring destruction without purpose.

If you cannot face Him,

you have no right to claim yourself as My Priestess.

Heru had to face Him.

Heru had to face the Great of Strength

in order to earn His Power.

One only earns Set's Power.

It is never given.

But one cannot claim the throne

without first claiming His Power.

Like My Power,

Set's Power is of transformation.

His is one of strength and endurance.

Mine is one of knowing yourself through your souls.

You need both in order to be a Priest or Priestess.

Heru needs both in order to be King.

A King of Two Lands.

Egypt is made of Two Lands.

Twin Souls must align in order to become whole.

Wesir must be broken to be made whole again.

Heru must give the Rejuvenating Eye to His Father

to make Him whole.

Do you understand?

You are Wesir.

Broken.

Dying.

You are Heru.

Rejuvenated Wesir.

He is the successor.

He goes where all do.

He must know Himself.
Do you know who you are?
He must face Set.
He must face Me.
In order to be King,
He must pass both Our tests.
Or not at all.
He must pass the test of the *ka*,
the flaming fire of creation.
This is Magic.
This is Power.
Of Ancestors and Gods.
This is the flame of the Stars and Suns.
This you must pass first.
Then comes the heart.
The *Ib* is the Seat of Who You Are.
Your tears are here.
Your hopes.
Your dreams.
Your emotions.
This is the path of the Inundation.
Is the Water here over-flowing?
Is the Water here not enough?
Where do the Waters flow?
What do you nourish them with?
What do you feed them with?
Garbage?
Joy?
Hope triumphing over despair?
Where is the Horizon here?
Where is the Dawn?
Do you see?
Your *ka* is the Dawn here.

The Pillars of Ra are not just peaks.
They contain your heart.
They contain your *ka*.
This is the Sunrise.
This is your Star.
This is your inner Star.
This is your soul's fire.
When it rises from the water, it flows.
This is your *ka* flowing
from your heart to your body.
The heart pumps.
The blood flows.
The blood carries the *ka*.
of both Ancestors and Gods.
This is My Lesson.
Now here is Set's.
Doing is His Power.
Strength is His Lesson.
Do you know your limits?
Are you willing to push forward,
no matter your fear?
He cannot destroy you
if you do not let Him.
He will not break you.
You are no good if you are broken.
He will mold you.
You will become who you need to be
in order to get the job done.
You will become who you are.
Entropy will dissolve.
Fear will be cast down.
Strength will remain.
You become who you are.

You shine as a star.

And you become the Falcon at Dawn.

And this is My Flame now.

For I am the Throne.

And then you are ready to become My Priestess.

But remember, Child.

To come to Me, you must know who you are.

Priestly Duties

The People do not understand
They do not know what they are doing.
They do not know what a Priest is.
They do not know what they are doing.
You do.
Why aren't you telling them?
Why aren't they listening?
A Priest is a Servant of God.
This is not just an office.
This is not just a ritual.
Do you want to serve a God?
Do you want to serve a Goddess?
Or Two?
Do you know what this entails?
Do you truly understand?
Do you truly know?
Dear child, listen.
The Way of the Priest is one of commitment.
You do not get to opt out
just because you don't feel like it that day.
You made a commitment.
Do you not go to work,
if you casually do not feel like it?
No.
You do not.
So, why are you doing this with Us?
With Me?

I do not mean physical illness here.
I mean emotional whimsy.
Why are you a Priest, dear child?
Why are you a Priest?
Why did you make this commitment,
if you are not up for the task?
Why do you doubt what I am saying?
You, child.
Yes, you.
Why do you doubt that I am the Voice of God?
Speaking?
Words are My Magic.
I speak. Magic happens.
My Work gets done in the World.
Not by miracles.
Although these can happen.
But by Words.
By actions.
By deeds.
This is My Magic in the World.
Priests and Priestesses
are My Eyes
are My Hands
are My Ears
and are My Mouths
in the World.
This is what you do,
if you are a Priest of one of Us.
This does not restrict itself to ritual.
This is All The Time.
Every day.
The way you weave through the world
is through Me.

Through the God or Goddess of the Priest.
For Priests are the Hands of God.
This is not something they are understanding.
The People do not understand.
It is not just a ritual.
It is a way of Being.
Of moving through the World.
Of souls aligned with the God or Goddess
of their Priestly mantle.
This is how they weave through the World.
All the Worlds.
Do you understand, child?
Do you understand?
Your souls are aligned with your Parent or Parents.
This is how you weave through the World.
This is how you operate.
This is the One or Ones you most resonate with
on all levels.
Yes, personality too.
You do not get to choose.
We made you.
We choose you for this task.
Not the other way around.
You can come to Us, yes.
You can ask Us, yes.
But if you are not ready,
We will decline.
And if you are ready,
We will accept.
But child, just because you are chosen
does not mean the Work is done.
The Ritual will change you.
We will flow through you.

You will be Our Hands.
You will be Our Ears.
You will be Our Eyes.
You will be Our Mouths.
In the World.
And this will change you.
This is why you must know who you are
beforehand.
You must have a strong foundation
before you begin.
Know who you are and serve Us.
And We will Name you Our Priest.
If you cannot do this, child,
then step away and assess your priorities.
If We are not a priority, then you cannot be Our Priest.
If We are not a priority, then you cannot be Our Priestess.
This does not mean We don't love you.
We do.
We love you.
But if you are unable to do the job at this time,
then step down.
Step away and re-assess yourself.
Is this what you want?
Is this what you need?
Would you be happier doing something else?
We know you wish to succeed.
We know you wish to serve Us.
And you still can,
but you must know who you are
and assess your priorities
before you decide to take up the mantle of Priesthood.

Do not worry, child.
Do not be afraid.
We are with you all the way.

The Mantle of Priesthood

The First Maxim of being a Priest or Priestess is to Know Yourself
The Second is to Serve your Gods
What are you doing, dear child?
What are you doing?
You cast Us away and push Us aside.
You do not integrate Us into your life.
You leave Us in shrine as if We are only located there.
We are everywhere.
Let Us in.
Let Us in.
We are interwoven through the World
and through the lives of Our Priests.
We are everywhere.
Not just in shrine.
When it gets to be too much, tell Us.
When you need a break, let Us know.
These are your boundaries.
Know them and We will work within them.
A broken Priest serves no one.
A half-assed Priest serves none.
Know who you are and what you want.
Know who you are and what you want.
Know who you are and what you want.
In all you are
In all your parts
Align your souls.
Align your *ka*, *ba* and heart.

Align all the elements.
Align your souls in any way you can.
And know who you are.
If you have not forgiven yourself for past mistakes,
or purged your self-loathing or doubt or fear.
If you have not faced down the darkest parts of your souls,
ripped them from their roots
and burned them clean away
through flame;
If you have not cleansed or cleaned out your soul
through a flood of tears that drown your very heart
If you have not been through the crucible of Set,
or the transformation of Aset,
then how do you know who you are?
The ritual is not enough.
They do not know who they are in order to perform it.
They come to you asking
for this mantle, this job, this honor,
not knowing what it means.
Not knowing what it means.
Not knowing what is expected.
Not knowing what is being asked or accepted.
A weekend alone does not make you a Priest.
This is absurd.
How can one become a Priest in three days?
This is not enough.
They do not understand.
And I am done.
I am done.
I am done with accepting Priests with these low standards.
They do not know who they are.
They have not worshiped Me long enough
to know who they are.

And this is a task for those who honor Me
and for those who are My children.
You are not the Ancient Egyptians.
You are not prepared as they were to perform this task.
The ritual is not enough--it never was.
The House of Life taught them for years in ancient times.
You have done this in three days.
A weekend.
A short time.
This takes years to prepare for.
Years.
This is not enough.
Another has left the fold.
Another has fled the mantle
that We have bestowed upon them.
Because of whimsy or self doubt
or other tasks took precedence.
Or wanting to serve Us
and not knowing what to do,
and thinking Priesthood is the only answer.
It is not.
It is a vocation.
It is a calling.
It is a damn job.
And this is not something you can have,
if you do not know who you are.
And this is not something that you can leave
because of whimsy or self-doubt or other insecurities
that should have been purged
before you took on the mantle.
You took this mantle and threw it away.
Threw it back in Our faces.
Do not come to Us asking for Priesthood

if you do not know who you are.
If you have not been purged of the shadows in yourself,
If you have not gone through the crucible of Set,
Or My tears or flame~
then do not ask.
We will say no.
Not yes.
Not anymore.
We will say no.
This is enough.
You are not ancient Egyptians.
Stop acting like it!

Priestess Maker

What is the Work of this God?
She Who reveals the Mysteries
Of the Goddess of Many Names, of Many Forms?
What is the Work of this God?
Of Aset
The Mighty
Mother of God
Lady of the West
Mistress of the Pyramid
Owner of *Heka* and Ra's Name
What is Her work?
Is singing Her work?
Is dancing, is writing?
What brings you joy?
What fills you with awe?
What clouds your terror and transforms you?
What is the Work of My servant?
The Priest, the Priestess?
Do they do ritual?
Do they honor the Gods and the dead?
Do they honor Me in their actions?
Do they follow Ma'at?
Do they do the vocation, the calling for Me?
Do they serve Me in every aspect of their lives?
Do they put Me first
Before all others?
of their ethereal families?

Before other pantheons?
Before other deities?
I am First
For I am the Goddess of creation
Of stars and sun
Of the phases of My son and husband as the moon
I am the Goddess of the *ka* and of the heart
Those who place me
In their hearts
Flowing through their *ka*
Will receive My blessings
My favor
My all
And these are the words of the Priestess maker
And these are the words of the Lady of Priests
And these are the words of the Goddess
Who places the king upon His seat
Who places the king upon His throne
Just as I place the Priest and Priestess
In their roles, in their office
As My Servants

Path of the Priestess

Creating beauty is a part of your Vocation
Through jewelry, through art
Your path of a Priestess
Is one of the Priestess of the Stars
As the Solar Goddess
As the Star Sopdet
As the Ancestral Stars
These are all a part of your Vocation
This is why I have revealed these Mysteries to you
For your path is the one of renewal
Of ancestors
Of the *ka*
Of the cosmos
Revealing My Mysteries
Is only one part of your path
Guiding people to My path
is a larger part of your service to Me
And you can do this in many forms
Through websites
Through books
Through art
For I am in all these things
For I am the Goddess Who Connects Worlds
I am the Goddess of liminal spaces
For I am the twin of Nebet Het
As She is the twin of Me
And We are intertwined as the Lady of the West

Who is also the Goddess of Stars
For I am the Mother, and She is the Beloved
And I am the Star Goddess
With a cow hide
Holding a Menat
Beaded Necklace
Which brings beauty, creation
and renewal to the World
Going between Worlds
Is a part of your Vocation
As is thriving in this one
You can do this with jewelry and websites
And Oracle Readings
And you will succeed, My Daughter
Because you are following your ka
You are flowing with life-force
The Universe will grant you your wish
But, remember, Child
This is My gift
Do not squander it
Do not treat it lightly
This is My Gift
And what I give I can take away
So treasure it
Do not abuse it
And you are on your way
To become My Priestess
My servant, My lovely Daughter

Message of the Priest

This is the Message of the Priest
I want to know where you are going
I want to know where you have been
To be a Priest is to be
the Hand of a God or Goddess
in the World.
This takes Work, Commitment and Sacrifice
You cannot go to the game,
if you have not done the ritual in the morning.
You cannot go to the warehouse
if you have not done obeisance to the God.
What are you doing, dear child?
What are you doing?
Being a Priest is a holy task
It is not a ritual alone.
It is knowing who you are.
It is knowing your foundation.
Have you done the work the Gods have asked?
This works for all Priests not just Mine.
What are you doing, dear child?
What are you doing?
Why is it We have to ask you to do things
you should already be doing?
Why is it We have to ask you to give to Us?
Why do you not do this on your own?
Do you ask others before you give a gift?
If yes, why?

Do you ask them what they want?

Do you give it to them right away?

Or do you wait until you are able to do so?

This is fine.

This is just.

And wise to give a God what They desire.

But, child, dear child

Do not ask Us for things if you do not give offerings.

Do not ask Us to make you a Priest,

if you are unwilling to do the work.

Do We inconvenience you?

Do you only want to do the work,

when it is convenient for you?

We are not unreasonable Gods.

Do you know the task before you?

Did you do the Work

before you asked to become a Priest?

To be the Hand of a God you must know who you are.

You must do the work you have been assigned.

You must do the Work to know who you are.

Rituals enact change in yourself.

They transform you.

They change you.

This is a permanent change.

Once the change happens, you cannot go back.

The change cannot be undone.

There is no such thing as a retired Priest.

Even former Priests are still the Hands of Their Gods.

Do you understand, child?

Do you understand?

To be a Priest is to change your soul.

Your souls align differently because of your job.

And they align because you know who you are.

These are permanent changes.
They cannot be erased or undone.
Do not ask to be a Priest
if you are not willing to do the work.
It is work.
Not just a title.
Not just a ritual.
To be a Priest is a privilege, an honor.
A role bestowed by the Holy Powers you revere.
Why are you throwing it away, dear child?
Why are you throwing it away?
Don't cast Us aside.
Don't cast Us aside.
Once driven out, We will not return.
So child, dear child
Know who you are before you ask.
Ensure that you know this.
Take courses to know who you are beforehand.
We will not take Priests if they keep leaving Us.
Know who you are and what you want in your life.
Things change. People change.
We understand this.
But child, dear child
Know who you are
before you take on the Priest's Mantle
If you do not, We will make you.
We will make it so you cannot turn away.
You must look at yourself.
Examine yourself so you know who you are.
You do not understand what this entails.
You are not doing the work beforehand.
You do not know who you are.
Are you a writer?

Are you a priest?
Are you both?
Who are you?
What is your focus?
What is a priority in your life?
Dear child, dear child
To know who you are, you must look into yourself
You must glare down your darkest fears and shame
And the parts of your soul that you have damaged,
you must mend.
The parts of your soul that others have damaged,
you must heal.
Yes, even the parts you don't like.
You must look at it all.
All of your parts must be made whole.
Or you are not ready to become a Priest.
As I re-membered Wesir,
you must re-member yourself.
You must animate yourself
Feed your heart, Feed your *ka*
So that you can re-align your soul
Then you will know who you are.
Then you will know if you are a Priest or a Devotee
Is Priesthood something you want?
Is Priesthood something you desire?
Do We have Work for you?
If not, if not, then you do not need to do this task.
This job is a thankless one.
Many hours of Work.
This is Work.
Not a hobby.
Not a game.
Not a fad.

This is Holy Work.
If you cannot do the work, then please,
please do not become a Priest.
Make sure you know what you are getting into before you do so.
Make offerings.
Pray.
Ask Us what Our work is for you.
Ask Us and We will show you the way.
Give gifts
and Our blessings will flow.
Do the Work
and Our blessings will multiply.
Don't do the work and Our blessings will cease.
And now you know the way to Priesthood.

Those Who Would Be Priests

Priesthood calls those who wish to serve.
They wish to be of service to others and their Gods.
This takes work.
Ritual. Dedication. Refinement.
And this takes the alignment of the souls.
To be a Priest or Priestess you must be mended.
You must be made whole.
In order to do this work you must know who you are.
And this means confronting who you are.
In all your glory and in all your beauty,
as well as the darker parts that lay hidden buried
in fear, anxiety, doubt,
and things that keep you from yourself.
Things that keep you buried
from the light of your own star,
your own soul.
In order to become a Priest you must do this work first.
And if you do not, then be prepared for it afterward.
For no one who serves can escape themselves.
And no one who serves can escape Me.
For I am the One Who Mends.
Did I not bring back Wesir?
Did I not reassemble Him
so that He could be whole in the Duat as King?
Will I not reassemble you, My child?
What makes you think
I will not help you become who you are?

This is who I am.
I bring life to the lifeless.
I mend those who are broken.
I bring Light forth from Darkness.
I am Aset-Sopdet. I am the Star Goddess.
I shine in the Night Sky as My Mother.
I shine in the night sky as all the stars.
The stars are the sun of night.
I am the Stellar and Solar Goddess of both Night and Day.
I bring flame to those who need transformation.
I bring light to those who need life.
Through magic I do these things.
Through ritual transformation occurs.
Do not think you can come to My threshold unchanged.
I will make you who you are.
If you are a Priest be prepared for this.
If you are thinking of Priesthood, be aware of this.
For We do not let go of Priests so casually.
Those who are Mine will always be Mine.
Those who are Priests will must go through the transformation of Sopdet.
They will come forth-shining
and descend into darkness-transformed
with water and flame, with tears and starlight.
And they will come forth again-renewed, whole.
They will shine as a star reflecting their own inner light

PART X

The Goddess's Husband Wesir (Osiris)

I am Renewed

To the Children of Netjer:
I am Wesir.
I am the King of the Duat.
Not a plaything.
Not an award.
Not a reward.
I am the King of the Ancestors.
I am the King of their lives in the Duat.
This is Who I am.
I am the God of their afterlives.
For life after death comes from Me.
I am the King of the Ancestors.
Honoring them also honors Me.
Set up a shrine to honor Me:
with a statue, candle and incense,
if you must.
And water.
A bowl of water is on My shrine.
For I have many mouths to feed.
And honoring Me also honors them–the Dead.
And honoring Them also honors Me.
I am the King of the Ancestors.
I am the King of the Dead.
Honor Me.
As you honor any King.
With implements of power and prestige.
Regalia.

I am the King of the Ancestors.
I am the King of the Dead.
All who die come to Me.
For I am the King of the Ancestors.
And I am the King of the Dead.
Gold and lapis lazuli
Blues and Greens of the Nile
are sacred to Me.
For I am the God of the Nile and all Waters.
All come to rest with Me.
I drowned.
I died.
The Nile is My resting place.
And My Beloved's tears rejuvenate Me.
For I am the King of the Ancestors.
All who die, all who drown
come to Me.
And the river leads to the ocean and fields.
These are My domains.
For I am the Navigation God.
All boats are Mine.
All Navigators, All Seas.
This is where Sarapis and I meet.
For I am the King of All Waters,
including rain.
While He is the King of the Sea.
This is where We meet and collide.
This is Our syncretism.
Wesir-Sarapis is My name.
And I am the God of the Greeks and Romans
as well as the Egyptians.
Sarapis too is all these things.
Just Him.

And I.
We do these things.
We rule all the Waters on land and sea.
Rivers. Lakes. Ponds.
These are My domain.
Rain and water that is consumed
And water-libations are all Mine.
I am the God of All Waters.
I am the God of All Rain.
All rivers are Mine.
All lakes and streams.
These are My domains.
The land is sacred to Me as well.
I am a Land God.
Vegetation and crops are holy to Me.
I help them grow with the Waters of My Heavenly domain.
My Wife's tears, My Beloved's too
Create rain to feed those below.
Animals and People are fed.
And I am content.
The Sky is sacred to Me.
For this is where I reside.
The Duat is in the Sky.
The Sky at Night is My domain,
In My Mother Nut, who holds many stars, a multitude
I reside where She is.
For I am in the Duat.
The starry sky is My domain.
The Heavenly forces are under My command.
For I am Orion,
the heavenly constellation in the sky.
She follows Me.
Sopdet follows Orion.

She searches for Me in the Duat.

In the Sky, I weave the time of day,

For Orion appears and disappears with Sopdet.

The Sirius Star follows Me in My domain.

She weeps, I die

and I am renewed as She reappears.

And the Nile floods.

And I am renewed once more.

I am the Moon God as She is the Star Goddess.

My Wife rules the Heavens as the Luminous One.

as the Bright One.

She burns fiercely bright.

My face illumines the shadows as the moon reflects Her light.

The moon in the sky does not burn.

The moon in the sky, waits.

I wax and wane as the moon travels in the Heavens.

from New to Full.

I die and am renewed with the phases of the moon.

My son does as well for He is a moon God

as Aset is the Star Goddess.

As His mother, She gives birth to Him.

And Me.

For I am renewed through My son.

As all ancestors are renewed through their descendants,

through the *Ka* of the family lines.

And all are renewed through Me.

As I renew the Heavens, through the light reflected by the moon.

All of creation is renewed through Me.

As the dead rise and rest.

As the waters flow.

As rain pours down.

As libations are poured out.

As the stars come out at night.

As the moon waxes and wanes.
All are renewed through Me.
Through water.
Through rain.
Through the rivers, whose banks overflow,
Through Orion's journey with Sopdet
Through the moon's phases
All are renewed through Me.
I am the Moon God.
I am the River God.
I am the Water God.
I am the Rain God.
I am the Star God.
I am the Heavenly God.
I am the Ancestral God.
I am the Royal God.
All are renewed through Me.

My Wife

In the water
I lie
Inert
Erect
Is my Penis
You come to me, O wife
You made my inertness fail
I live again, O wife
Crops grow
Fields emerge
Moon, now full
I transformed
From man to King
By You
My wife

I am Wesir

I am Wesir
I am the God of the grains
The Mysteries of the Earth are My domain
For I am the son of the Earth God
My Mother is the starry sky
My wife as well
I reside within Their embrace
My Mother and My Beloved
Enfold Me in Their wings
Enfold Me in Their love
They protect Me and the stars above
For the stars are the ancestors
And I am their King
My sisters wait with Me
In the Hall of Judgment
So the deceased may be worthy of Paradise
I am the one in command here
I am the King
I merge with Ra
Our Father
So that the Inert can rise
So that the dead have a renewing light
A brush of life
They are renewed
As am I
And I am the only God
Who understands the pain of death

Who understands the transformation
All must go through in order to enter My Hall
In order to pass judgment
I must know what each has gone through
I know the sorrows of My wife and sister
I know because all the dead
Mourn for what they had to leave behind
They have to let go of the lives and loved ones
they left in the Seen World
This is the sorrow I understand
This is the sorrow I know
I know the pain of letting go
For I am the only God to die
I am the Green God
I share the Mysteries of the Earth
With My Father and My wife
My Beloved is the Green Goddess
Just as I am the Green God
I bring life to death and back again
I am the God of Renewal
Plants grow and die
Only to spread their seed
And grow again
This is the Mystery of Renewal
This is the Mystery I possess
This is the Mystery of Wesir

Ascension

I am Wesir
I am the God of Kings
I am the God of the Dead
They honor Me
and I honor them
They are the transfigured dead
These are the people who have died,
and go through the Gates of the Underworld.
They made it to My Hall
and passed My Judgment in the Hall of Ma'ati.
My Hall is of My Sister and Wife
Nebet Het (Nephthys) and Aset (Isis) rule alongside Me here.
They are the Two Truths, the Ma'ati.
The Twin Sisters of both life and death.
They are the judgment.
They judge the dead
and name their names
and their deeds and their actions
and their desires.
Your life is judged by these measures.
Act.
Act.
Do the things you love, which makes your heart sing
Do the things you desire, for that will feed your *ka*
and the *kau* of your ancestral dead.

Do the things you need, to feed yourself
so that you may come to My Hall
assured in your ascension
to be among the Blessed Dead.

To Become a Transfigured Spirit

This is My time
The time of Wesir
This is My crucible
Death of the God,
who had died.
Death is not the end.
It is a beginning
of a new transition,
into a spiritual body
made up of the alignment of your souls
Ib, Ka and *Ba.*
The heart (*Ib*) is the center of yourself,
your wants and desires.
The *ka* is your vital essence,
which flows throughout your body
and enables you to live
do magic
and connect to your dead.
The *ba* is your ethereal body,
the one which walks in the Unseen Realm
and interacts with the Gods and those of the Duat.
When these souls are aligned,
you become a Transfigured Spirit,
you are a member of the dead,
who has been justified.
You are found wanting things

which you don't achieve.
You waste My time
begging for things you do not need,
or want or desire.
Why do you do this?
Why do you bend your will to fit those around you?
Why do you bend your will to honor others,
but not yourself?
Why do you bend your will to honor
those who don't honor you?
Why do you let people trample over your feet?
This is your path.
This is your life.
The choices you make effect not only the living,
but the dead.
And these choices you make effect all those you
come into contact with.
And the choices you make challenge you
to become a transfigured spirit.

Wesir and Nut

I am Wesir
I aid the disenfranchised
I aid the downtrodden
I aid those who ask
for Me to help them.
This is Who I am.
I am like My Mother, Nut
She is the Mother of All
And I am the Father of All,
as I am Wesir, the Lord of the Dead.
The Duat is My home,
within My Mother, Nut.
I aid the disenfranchised
I aid those who call upon Me.
I am like My Mother, Nut,
the starry sky,
the Queen of Heaven,
the Lady of the West,
as the One Who holds the stars
in Her embrace.
This is My Mother Nut.
I am like Nut.
I am the Lord of Stars.
I am the Lord of Heaven.
I am the Lord of the West.
I am like My Mother, Nut.
I aid the disenfranchised.

I aid those who call upon Me.
Yes, child,
even you.

Wesir and Geb

I am Wesir
I am like My Father Geb
I am the stones of the oasis
I am encased in earth
as He is.
The Lord of the West,
rules over where they are buried.
Geb is the Lord of the Necropolis,
Graves are His because they are of the land.
As am I, as Lord of the Graves and the West.
Secrets are buried here,
within the earth.
Stones and minerals,
plants and food.
This all comes from Me
and My Father Geb.
As Lord of the Land
We rule over generations
of rulers, of farmers
of every kind of devotee
of every kind of person,
We rule them all.
For My Father is Lord and King,
as much as I.
For I inherited His throne,
when I was alive.

Geb is the King of the Land
as am I.
I rule over all,
as King.

Wesir and Ra

I am Wesir
as Lord of Heaven,
like My Father, Ra.
He shines
I reflect His light in the moon.
For I am parallel to Him.
For I am His counterpart
in the Duat.
He is the Day,
I am the Night.
I shine brightly,
when I reflect His light.
This not a passive role.
This is an active one.
Have you ever tried to reflect light?
I triangulate the path of sunbeams
I hold fast,
as the scorching heat and flames
bear down on Me.
Yet, I reflect His light.
To shine down on everyone.
And this is a type of renewal
For the light from the sun
also renews Me.
As I am renewed,
so too is the cosmos.
I am Lord of the Moon

because it is a source of renewal
through its phases
and reflected light,
shining as bright in the night.
I am Wesir, Lord of Light
I reflect the light of the King of the Gods
My Father Ra, Lord of Sunbeams.
I am Wesir,
who joins with Ra in the Duat
when He shines for the dead
to rejuvenate Me
and the cosmos as well.
For this is My role.
I take power and reflect it back.
I shape it and mold it,
and send it back.
For I share the power that is given to Me,
by others.
For I am Wesir, Lord of the People.

Sopdet and Orion

Wesir: Fiercely Bright One
is the name of the Goddess
and the God.
I am Fiercely Bright in the Duat
as a Star, as Orion
While My Wife is Fiercely Bright
as Sopdet, the star Sirius in the Sky,
within the Duat.
within Me.
Sopdet follows Orion.
Sopdet within the course of Orion.
This is where We meet.
I am the Star of the Nighttime sky
She is the Star of the Daytime sky
We meet at the Horizon.
We meet at the apex in the sky.
She renews Me
and the cosmos is renewed
as Sopdet and Orion.

Aset: I am Sopdet
He is Orion.
When I am Fiercely Bright
I am the Solar Goddess of the Day
and the Star Goddess of the Nighttime Sky
This is Who I am as the Fiercely Bright One.
I am the Solar Goddess of the Dawn

I am the Star Goddess of the Night.
All stars are Mine.
I am Fiercely Bright.
I am the sun.
I am the stars.
Burning Bright.
I am the Goddess of the Day
I am the Goddess of the Night.
I always burn Fiercely Bright
on the days and nights
of My solar and stellar festivals,
and when I follow My husband in the Heavens.
I am Sopdet.
He is Orion.
We are Fiercely Bright.

Wesir: I am Fiercely Bright
as the star Orion,
in the Duat.

Aset: I am the star Sopdet,
as I follow Orion in the Heavens.
And I am the Star Goddess here,
following My husband
in the Duat.
Together and always.

Wesir: I am Lord of the Duat,
I am Lord of the Night
The Moon is My symbol
as it waxes and wanes.
This is Me as Lord of the Night.

Aset: I am the Lady of the Duat
I am the gold dust of stars
burning in the night.
I am the Star Goddess, Fiercely Bright.
I am Sopdet, who renews My husband,
This is Me as Lady of the Night.

Together: We are the Lord and Lady of the Duat.
We are the Lady and Lord of the Night.
We are stars, burning bright.
We are Fiercely Bright
as the Star Goddess and Star God,
Lord and Lady,
Fiercely Bright.

Star Lord

Star Lord
Star God
This is Who I am
as Orion.
I am the King of the Duat.
I am the Lord of the River in the Sky.
I am the Lord of the Stars.
I am a King as My Wife is a Queen.
She is the Dog Star
I am Orion, the constellation of stars.
I rise before My Wife
on the New Year.
And She follows Me.
And all is renewed,
as She is the Star Goddess
and I am the Star Lord.

Dog-Star

Stars are small suns
They shine in the sky as brightly as Ra,
the Sun God.
They shine and We call those who honor Us.
To Our Mysteries of the Mothers and Fathers
To Our Mysteries of the *Ka*,
With Our son,
the Wolf Lord and to the Lord of All.
Wepwawet (Ophois) and Yinepu (Anubis),
for They are Our sons,
in the Duat.
They are Guides and Guardians.
They guide souls and guard them from harm,
on their journey home.
They are what the Greeks called Psychopompos,
the Guide of Souls in the Duat.

Do you wonder why Sopdet is the Dog Star?
She is the Queen of Canines.
Dogs, Hounds and Wolves
Foxes and Coyotes
They are all Hers.
For they guide and guard the Dead.
For they hunt and track,
while searching for Me,
who is Wesir.

They destroy evil,
Tearing with their claws
Gnashing with their teeth,
they tear the evil doers asunder.
They protect the Weary-of-Heart,
the one called Wesir, their Father.
They protect Aset as well,
for She is their Mother.
And this is why My Lady is the Dog-Star,
For She travels, searching for Me
with Her sons,
the Wolf Lord and the Lord of All.

PART XI

Songs of the Goddess

Song of the Bright Ones

To Aset: Brightest of Stars
Why don't you know,
who you are?
Lady of Lights
Come join us tonight
Goddess of Stars
You know who You are
Lady so Bright
Join Us tonight
See the glow of the flame
on the candles so bright!
Let the candles burn,
Let there be light!
Oh, Lady, Lady
Burning so Bright!
Lady, Lady
Let there be Light!
Lady, Lady
Burning so bright
Lady, Lady
Let there be light!

To Wesir: Lord of Stars,
burning so bright.
Lord of Orion,
join us tonight!
Lord, Lord
Orion so bright,
Please join Your Lady,
Please join us tonight!
Let there be music,
Let there be light!
Please join the chorus,
join us tonight!
Please join the Lady,
Burning so bright!
Come to the altar
Come to the shrine,
Burning so bright
Please join us
as we light candles
on this very night.
Come to Your altar,
Come to Your shrine,
Join Your Lady
Who is divine.
Please join the chorus,
Please enjoy the wine!
Come join the chorus,
please Lord Divine!
Come join the Lady,
Come join the Lord,
Blessings flow
when They are adored!

Song of the Lady and Lord

Please join the Lady,
Please join the Lord,
Please join the Lady,
Where They are ever adored!

Come join the festival,
Come drink the wine!
Come to Your altar,
Holy and Divine!

Let there be music
Let there be light,
Play the sistra,
on this holy night!

Come join the Lady,
Come join the Lord,
Let there be music,
as They are adored!

Come join the Lady,
Come join the Lord,
Come join the Lady
as They are ever adored!

Come join the worship
Come join the dance,

Come join the festival
and be entranced!

Call to the Lady,
Call to the Lord,
Call to the Lady,
as They are ever adored!

Come join the music
Come join the dance,
Come join the Lady,
and be entranced!

Come join the Lady,
Come join the Lord,
Come join the Gods
as They are ever adored!

Goddess of the River

Goddess of Rivers,
Goddess of Life,
Goddess of Rivers,
on this Holy Night!

Come join the Circle,
Come join the rite!
Come join the Circle,
on this Holy Night!

God of the River,
God of the Light
God of the River,
on this Holy Night!

Come join the Circle,
Come join the rite!
Come join the Circle,
on this Holy Night!

Goddess of Rivers,
Goddess of Life,
Come with Your Lord
on this Holy night.

Come join the Circle,
Come join the rite!

Come join the Circle,
on this Holy Night!

Lady of Rivers,
Lady of Life,
Lord of the Waters,
Come join us tonight!

Come join the Circle,
Come join the rite!
Come join the Circle,
on this Holy Night!

Lord of the River,
Lady of Life,
Lord and the Goddess,
Please join us tonight!

Burning Bright

Please join the Circle,
Please join the rite.
Please join the Circle
on this holy night.

Goddess of Rivers,
Goddess so Bright,
Lady of Stars,
Please join us tonight!

Please join the Circle,
Please join the rite.
Please join the Circle
on this holy night.

Goddess of Rivers,
Goddess so Bright,
Lady of Stars,
Shining with Light.

Please join the Circle,
Please join the rite.
Please join the Circle
on this holy night.

Lady of Candles,
Burning so bright,
Goddess of Stars,
Lady of Light

Please join the Circle,
Please join the rite.
Please join the Circle
on this holy night.

Goddess of Rivers,
Lady of Light,
Goddess of Candles,
Burning so bright.

Please join the Circle,
Please join the rite.
Please join the Circle
on this holy night.

Goddess of Rivers,
Lady of Streams
Goddess of Stars
Send your sunbeams.

Please join the Circle,
Please join the rite.
Please join the Circle
on this holy night.

Goddess of Ladies

Goddess of Ladies,
Goddess so Bright,
Goddess of Ladies
Join us tonight.

Dance with the Ladies
Dance with the Lords
Dance for the Goddess
and libations are poured.

Goddess of Ladies,
Goddess so Bright
Lady of Incense
Join us tonight.

Goddess of Ladies,
Goddess so Bright,
Goddess of Ladies
Join us tonight.

Goddess of Ladies
Goddess of Light
Goddess of Ladies
Burning so bright.

Goddess of Ladies,
Goddess so Bright,
Goddess of Ladies
Join us tonight.

Dance for the Mother
Whirling around
Dance for the Mother
And you'll always be found.

Goddess of Ladies,
Goddess so Bright,
Goddess of Ladies
Join us tonight.

Playing the sistrum
Goddess so Bright
May this appease You
on this holy night.

Goddess of Ladies,
Goddess so Bright,
Goddess of Ladies
Join us tonight.

Called

Lady of Rivers
Lady of Lords
Lady of Rivers
and libations are poured.

Goddess of Candles
Burning so bright
Lady of Flame
Burning all through the night.

Goddess of Water
Goddess of Streams
Look very closely
and you'll see what I mean.

Goddess of Rivers,
Goddess of Rain
All who know Me
Know of My pain.

I am the Goddess
He is the God
I am the Goddess
You will be called.

Goddess of Rivers,
Goddess of Might,
Bright and Fierce Lady,
Join us tonight.

Come to the Goddess
Come to the God,
Join in the Circle
You will be called.

Lady of Rivers,
Lady of Light
Burning, Bright Lady
Please join us tonight.

Mystery and Magic

I am the Lady
He is the Lord
I am the Lady
Libations are poured.

I am the Lady
I am the Queen
I am the Lady
Ruler of Sunbeams.

I am the Lady
He is the Lord
I am the Lady
Libations are poured.

I am the Lady
I am the Queen
Come to the Goddess
Glowing bright blue and green.

Goddess and Lady
Goddess of Light
Share with us, Lady
Your Mysteries tonight.

Come to the Goddess
Come to the God
Come to us, Lady,
with Your golden rod.

Come to the Goddess
Come to the God
Libations are made
and all applaud.

Come to the Goddess
Learn of Her well
Come to the Goddess,
She Who knows Her spells.

Lady of Magic
Lady of Might
Lady of *Ka*-Power
Come to us this night!

Lady of Magic
Of Mysteries I speak,
Come to the Lady
and She will entreat-

Lady of Magic
Lady of Life
The Mysteries are revealed
by You, tonight.

Come to the Lady
Come all who seek,
Come to hear the words
of the Lady who speaks.

I speak of enchantment
for those who will hear
I speak of the Mysteries
Lend Me your ear.

I am the Goddess
He is the God
I am the Lady
who wields the golden rod.

Lady of enchantment
Mysteries I seek
Lady of Magic
to You I entreat.

Goddess of Mercy
Goddess so Sweet
Lady of Magic
to you I entreat

Goddess and Lady
Glorious and Divine
Goddess and Lady
Forever be Mine.

Come be enchanted
Come be enthralled
Listen to the Lady
for She knows all.

Listen to the Lady
Listen to the Lord
Listen to the Gods
Libations are poured.

They teach Mysteries
to all those who seek.
They teach the Mysteries
to the wise and the meek.

Come to the Lady
Come to the Lord
Come to the Lady
where libations are poured.

They teach the Mysteries
to all those who ask
They teach the Mysteries
Are you ready to reveal your mask?

Come to the Lady
Come to the Lord
Come to the Lady
libations are poured.

They teach the Mysteries
to all those who seek
at the end of the lesson,
the seeker will no longer be meek.

Come to the Shrine

Come to the Lady
and the Lord Divine
Come to the Gods
and go to Their shrine.

I call the Lady
I call the Lord
I call the Gods
where libations are poured.

Come to the Lady
Come to the Lord
Come to the temple
where They are adored.

Candles burn brightly
Lady of Life
Candles burn brightly
all through the night.

Vigilant Lady
Guarding Her shrine
Guiding Lady
Serene and Divine

Come to the Lady
Come to the Shrine
Guardian Lady
Peaceful and Divine

Come to the Lady
Come to the Lord
Come to all places
where They are adored.

Come to the Goddess
Come to the Lord
Come to the Lady
where They are adored.

Run to the Goddess
Run to the God
Beautiful Lady
Stalwart and Strong

Here is the Goddess
Here is the God
Lady of Life
Here you are awed.

Goddess of Ladies
Goddess of Lords
Lady of Weaving
Who is always adored.

Beautiful Lady

Beautiful Lady
Goddess of Life
Beautiful Lady
She is His Wife.

Beautiful Lady
Goddess of Streams
Beautiful Lady
Lady of Sunbeams.

Beautiful Lady
Beautiful Life
Beautiful Lady
Beautiful Wife.

Goddess of Children
Rivers and Streams
Goddess of the People
Who pours out sunbeams7.

Beautiful Lady
Beautiful Life
Beautiful Lady
She is My wife.

Wife of Wesir
Wife of the Lord
Wife of the Savior
She is greatly adored.

Goddess and Savior
Goddess of Life
Goddess and Lady
She is My wife.

Song of the Brightest of Ladies

Brightest of Ladies
Brightest of Lights
Come, join the Circle
Come join the rite!

Light the incense,
Burn the candles
Offer to the Goddess
On this night!

Pour out libations
Pour out the wine
Give to the Gods,
and you'll always be fine.

Brightest of Ladies,
Brightest of Lights
Come, join the circle
Come, join the rite!

Thank the Lady
Thank the Lords.
Thank the Lady,
Libations are poured.

Lady of Rivers,
Lady of Light

Lady of Waters,
Shine through the night!

Brightest of Ladies,
Brightest of Lights
Come, join the circle
Come, join the rite!

Give to the Lady,
She knows Her spells
Give to the Lady
and all will be well.

Brightest of Ladies
Brightest of Lights
May You be blessed
on this Holy Night!

PART XII

Epilogue

References

- Allen, T. G. The Book of the Dead or Going Forth By Day: Ideas of the Ancient Egyptians concerning the hereafter as expressed in their own terms. Oriental Institute of the University of Chicago, Studies in Ancient Oriental Civilization #37, 1974.
- Altenmüller, Hartwig. "Feste." Lexikon der Ägyptologie Gotter und Gotterbezeichnungen. volume 2. ed. Wolfgang Helck and Wolfhart Westendorf. (Columns 171-191). Ortiz Harrassowitz, 1977.
- Alvar, Jaime. Romanising Oriental Gods: Myth, Salvation and Ethics in the Cults of Cybele, Isis and Mithras. Brill Academic Pub, 2008.
- Andrews, Carol. Amulets of Ancient Egypt. Texas: University of Texas Press, 1994.
- Apuleius. The Golden Ass or the Metamorphoses. translated by E. J. Kenney. Penguin Classics, 2004.
- Arslan, Ermanno, ed. Iside: Il mito, il mistero, la magia. Milan: Electa, 1997.
- Assmann, Jan. The Search for God in Ancient Egypt. Translated by David Lorton. Ithaca: Cornell University Press, 2001.
- Assmann, Jan. The Mind of Egypt. Translated by Andrew Jenkins. New York: Metropolitan Books, 1996.
- Bakir, Abd el-Mohsen. The Cairo Calendar No. 86637. Cairo, 1966.
- Baring, Anne and Jules Cashford. "Isis of Egypt: Queen of Heaven, Earth and the Underworld". The Myth of the

Goddess: Evolution of an Image. Anne Baring and Jules Cashford, ed. New York: Penguin, 1993, pp. 225-272.

- Baedeker, Karl. Egypt: Upper Egypt with Nubia as far as the Second Cataract and the Western Oases. Dulau and Co., 1892.

- Beard, Mary and North, John and Simon Price. Religions of Rome: Volume 2: A Sourcebook. Cambridge University Press, 1998.

- Bergman, Jan. Ich Bin Isis: Studien zum memphitischen Hintergrund der griechischen Isisaretalogien. Almquist & Wiksell, Uppsalla, 1968.

- Betz, Hans Dieter. The Greek Magical Papyri: In Translation including the Demotic Spells, Vol 1. London: The University of Chicago Press, 1996.

- Bibliotheca Alexandrina. Waters of Life: A Devotional Anthology for Isis and Serapis. Buchanan, Rebecca and Jeremy H. Baer, ed. Bibliotheca Alexandrina, 2009.

- Blackman, Aylward M. Gods, Priests and Men. New York: Kegan Paul International, 1998.

- Blackman, Aylward M. The Temple of Dendur. Cairo: Dar al-Maaref, 1981; 1911.

- Bell, Lanny. "The New Kingdom Divine Temple: The Example of Luxor," in Temples of Ancient Egypt, ed. Byron E. Shafer, New York: Cornell University Press, 1997.

- Bleeker, C. J. "Isis and Hathor: Two Egyptian Goddesses" in The Book of the Goddess Past and Present: An Introduction to Her Religion. Ed. By Carl Olson. New York: Crossroad Publishing, 1986.

- Bleeker, C. J. Egyptian Festivals: Enactments of Religious Renewal. E. J. Brill, Publishers, 1967.

- Bleeker, C. J. "Isis and Nephthys as Wailing Women". Numen 5 (1958), pp. 1-17.

- Bleeker, C. J. "Isis as Saviour Goddess," in S. G. F. Brandon, ed. The Saviour God: Comparative Studies in the Concept of Salvation. New York: Barnes and Noble, (1963), pp. 1-16.
- Boheme, Marie-Ange. "Divinity." Translated by Elizabeth Schwaiger. In Ancient Gods Speak: A Guide to Egyptian Religion. edited by Donald Redford. New York: Oxford University Press, 2002, pp. 106-112.
- Bolton, Chelsea Luellon. Lady of Praise, Lady of Power: Ancient Hymns of the Goddess Aset. Lulu Press, 2016.
- Borghouts, J. L. Ancient Egyptian Magical Texts. E. J. Brill Leiden, 1978.
- Borghouts, J. F. "The Evil Eye of Apopis," in The Journal of Egyptian Archaeology, Vol. 59 (Aug., 1973), pp. 114-150.
- Bresciani, E. and S. Pernigotti. Il tempio tolemaico di Isi ad Assuan. Pisa: Giardini Editori E. Stampatori, 1978.
- Britcault, Laurent. "Isis Nepherses" in Egyptian Religion: The Last Thousand Years Part 1: Studies Dedicated to the Memory of Jan Quaegebeur. edited by Willy Clarysse, Antoon Schoors and Harco Willems. Peeters, 1998, pp. 522-527.
- Bricault, Laurent. "Un trône pour deux." Mythos. Numero 3, n. s., 2009, pp. 131-142.
- Bricault, Laurent. "La diffusion isiaque: une esquisse." Fremdheit-Eigenheit. Ägypten, Griechenland und Rom. Austausch und Verständnis (2004): 548-556.
- Bricault, Laurent. "Du nom des images d'Isis polymorphe." C. Bonnet, J. Rüpke et P. Scarpi (éd.), Religions orientales-culti misterici. Neue Perspektiven-nouvelles perspectives-prospettive nuove (2006): 75-94.
- Bricault, Laurent. "Un phare, une flotte, Isis, Faustine et l'annone." Chronique d'Egypte 75, no. 149 (2000): 136-149.
- Bricault, Laurent. "Isis dolente." Bulletin de l'Institut français d'archéologie orientale 92 (1992): 37-49.

- Bricault, Laurent. Isis, dame des flots. Volume 7 Ægyptiaca Leodiensia. C.I.P.L, 2006.
- Bricault, Laurent. Recueil des Inscriptions Concernant les Cultes Isiaques: Vol. 1. Académie des Inscriptions et Belles-Lettres, 2005.
- Bricault, Laurent. Recueil des Inscriptions Concernant les Cultes Isiaques: Vol. 2. Académie des Inscriptions et Belles-Lettres, 2005.
- Bricault, Laurent and Miguel John Versluys, ed. Isis on the Nile: Egyptian Gods in Hellenistic and Roman Egypt: Proceedings of the IVth International Conference of Isis Studies, Liege, November 27-29, 2008. Brill Academic Pub, 2010.
- Bricault, Laurent, Miguel John Versluys and Paul G. P. Meyboom, ed. Nile into Tiber: Egypt in the Roman World: Proceedings of the IIIrd International Conference of Isis Studies, Leiden, May 11-14 2005. Brill, 2007.
- Bricault, Laurent, ed. Power, Politics and the Cults of Isis: Proceedings of the Vth International Conference of Isis Studies, Boulogne-sur-Mer, October 13-15, 2011. (Religions in the Graeco-Roman World). Brill Academic Publishers, 2014.
- Bricault, Laurent. Les Cultes Isiaques Dans Le Monde Greco-romain (La Roue a Livres / Documents Book 66). Les Belles Lettres, 2013.
- Brier, Bob. Ancient Egyptian Magic. New York: William Morrow and Company, 1980.
- Bryan, Betsy M. "The Temple of Mut: New Evidence on Hatshepsut's Building Activity". in Roehrig, Catharine H., Cathleen A. Keller, and Renée Dreyfus (eds). *Hatshepsut: from Queen to Pharaoh.* New York, The Metropolitan Museum of Art; New Haven, Yale University Press, 2005.

- Budzanowski, Mikolaj. "Isis, Harpocrates, and the Lion Throne." in Popielska-Grzybowska, Joanna (ed.), <u>Proceedings of the First Central European Conference of Young Egyptologists, Egypt 1999. (Warsaw University, 2001), Volume 3</u>, pp. 14-20.
- Buhl, Marie-Louise. "The Goddesses of the Egyptian Tree Cult," *The Journal of Near Eastern Studies*, Vol. 6, No. 2 (Apr., 1947), 80-97.
- Bumbaugh, Solange. "Meroitic Worship of Isis at Philae". in <u>Egypt in its African Context: Proceedings of the conference held at The Manchester Museum, University of Manchester, 2-4 October 2009</u>. edited by Karen Exell. Archaeopress, 2011.
- Capel, Anne K. and Glenn E. Markoe, ed. <u>Mistress of the House, Mistress of Heaven: Women in Ancient Egypt</u>. New York: Hudson Hills Press, 1996.
- Capron, Laurent. "Déclarations fiscales du Temple de Soknopaiou Nêsos: éléments nouveaux," in <u>Zeitschrift für Papyrologie und Epigraphik</u>. Bd. 165, Dr. Rudolf Habelt GmbH, Bonn (Germany). (2008), pp. 133-160.
- Cauville, Sylvie. <u>Dendara I: Traduction</u>. Peeters, 1998.
- Cauville, Sylvie. <u>Dendara II: Traduction</u>. Peeters, 1999.
- Cauville, Sylvie. <u>Dendara III: Traduction</u>. Peeters, 2000.
- Cauville, Sylvie. <u>Dendara IV: Traduction</u>. Peeters, 2001.
- Cauville, Sylvie. <u>Dendara V-VI: Traduction. Les Cryptes du Temple d'Hathor. Vol. I</u>. Peeters, 2004.
- Cauville, Sylvie. <u>Dendara V-VI. Les Cryptes du Temple d'Hathor. Vol. II</u>. Orientalia Lovaniensia Analecta, Peeters, 2004.
- Cauville, Sylvie<u>. Dendara VIII: Les Fetes d'Hathor</u>. Peeters, 2002.
- Cauville, Sylvie. <u>Dendara XIII: Traduction</u>. Peeters, 2011.
- Cauville, Sylvie. <u>Dendara XIV: Traduction</u>. Peeters, 2011.

- Cauville, Sylvie. <u>Dendara XV: Traduction: Pronaos de Temple d'Hathor</u>. Peeters, 2012.
- Cauville, Sylvie. <u>La Temple de Dendara: La Porte d'Isis</u>. Institut Francais d'Archeologie Orientale, 1999.
- Cauville, Sylvie. <u>Dendara: Le Temple de Isis. Vol 1</u>. Traduction. Orientalia Lovaniensia Analecta, Peeters, 2009.
- Cauville, Sylvie. <u>La Temple de Dendara: La Chapelles de Osiriennes: Translation et Traduction</u>. Institut Francais d'Archeologie Orientale, 1997.
- Cauville, Sylvie. <u>Offerings to the Gods in Egyptian Temples</u>. translated by Bram Calcoen. Peeters, 2012.
- Clark, R. T. Rundle. <u>Myth and Symbol in Ancient Egypt</u>. New York: Thames and Hudson, 1959.
- Coppens, Filip. <u>The Wabet: Tradition and Innovation in Temples of the Ptolemaic and Roman Period</u>. Prague: Czech Institute of Egyptology, 2007.
- Corrington, Gail Paterson. "The Milk of Salvation: Redemption by the Mother in Late Antiquity and Early Christianity." *The Harvard Theological Review, Vol. 82, No. 4 (Oct., 1989)*, pp. 393-420.
- Corsu, France Le. <u>Isis: Mythe et Mysteres (Collection d'Etudes Mythologiques)</u>. Paris: Societe d'Edition Les Belles Lettres, 1977.
- Coulon, Laurent. "Les formes d'Isis à Karnak à travers la prosopographie sacerdotale de l'époque ptolémaïque," <u>Isis on the Nile: Egyptian Gods in Hellenistic and Roman Egypt: Proceedings of the IVth International Conference of Isis Studies, Liege, November 27-29, 2008.</u> Bricault, Laurent and Miguel John Versluys, ed. Brill Academic Pub, 2010.
- Coyle, T. Thorn. <u>Kissing the Limitless: Deep Magic and the Great Work of Transforming Yourself and the World</u>. Red Wheel/Weiser Books, 2009.

- Coyle, T. Thorn. Make Magic of Your Life: Purpose, Passion and the Power of Desire. Red Wheel/Weiser Books, 2013.
- Darnell, John Coleman. "Apotropaic Goddess in the Eye," Studein zur Altagyptischen Kultur, Bd. 24 (1997), pp. 35-48.
- David, Rosalie. A Guide to Religious Ritual at Abydos. Warminster: Aris and Phillips, 1981.
- David, Rosalie. Religion and Magic in Ancient Egypt. New York: Penguin Books, 2002.
- Dennis, James Teackle. Burden of Isis: Being the Laments of Isis and Nephthys. London: J. Murray, 1918.
- De Jong, Aleid. "Feline Deities," in Ancient Gods Speak: A Guide to Egyptian Religion, ed. Donald Redford: New York: Oxford University Press, 2002, pp. 123-124.
- Dijkstra, Jitse H. F. Philae and the End of Ancient Egyptian Religion: A Regional Study of Religious Transformation (298-642 CE). Peeters, 2008.
- Dijkstra, Jitse H. F. and Eugene Cruz-Uribe. Syene I: the figural and textual graffiti from the temple of Isis at Aswan. Phillip von Zabern, 2012.
- Donalson, Malcolm Drew. The Cult of Isis in the Roman Empire: Isis Invicta. New York: Edwin Mellen Press, 2003.
- Dousa, Thomas. "Praising Isis in Demotic." in The Bulletin of the American Society of Papyrologists (BASP) Vol. 47 (2010), pages 241-253.
- Doxey, Denise M. "Nephthys." in Ancient Gods Speak: A Guide to Egyptian Religion. edited by Donald Redford. New York: Oxford University Press, 2002, pp. 275-276.
- Dunand, Francoise. Le Culte d'Isis dans le Bassin Oriental de la Mediterranee Vol 1: Le Culte d'Isis et les Ptolemees. Brill Academic Publishers, 1973.

- Dunand, Francoise. <u>Le Culte d'Isis dans le Bassin Oriental de la Mediterranee Vol 2: Le Culte d'Isis en Grece</u>. Brill Academic Publishers, 1973.

- Dunand, Francoise. <u>Le Culte d'Isis dans le Bassin Oriental de la Mediterranee Vol 3: Le Culte d'Isis en Asie Mineure Clerge et Rituel des Sanctuaires Isiaques</u>. Brill Academic Publishers, 1973.

- Dunand, Francoise. <u>Isis, Mere Des Dieux</u>. Babel Actes Sud, 2008.

- DuQuesne, Terence. <u>The Salakhana Trove: Votive Stelae and Other Objects from Asyut</u>. London: Darengo Publications, 2009.

- DuQuesne, Terence. <u>Anubis, Upwawet and Other Deities: Personal Worship and Official Religion in Ancient Egypt</u>. The Egyptian Museum of Cairo, 2008.

- DuQuesne, Terence. "Exalting the God: Processions of Upwawet in Asyut in the New Kingdom". *Discussions in Egyptology, Vol. 57.* 2003, pp. 21-46.

- DuQuesne, Terence. "The Great Goddess and her Companions in Middle Egypt". *'Mythos und Ritual. Festschrift für Jan Assmann zum 70. Geburtstag.'* 2008.

- Durdin-Robertson, Lawrence. <u>Juno Covella: Perpetual Calendar of the Fellowship of Isis</u>. Cesara Publications, 1975; 1982.

- Ellis, Normandi. <u>Feasts of Light: Celebrations for the Seasons of Life based on the Egyptian Goddess Mysteries</u>. Quest Books, 1999.

- El-Sabban, Sherif. <u>Temple Festival Calendars of Ancient Egypt</u>. Wiltshire: Liverpool University Press, 2000.

- el-Saddy, Hassan. "Reflections on the Goddess Tayet", in *The Journal of Egyptian Archeaology Vol 80*, 1994, 213-217.

- Englund, Gertie. "Offerings." in <u>Ancient Gods Speak: A Guide to Egyptian Religion</u>. edited by Donald Redford. New York: Oxford University Press, 2002, pp. 279-290.

- El-Saghir, Mohamed and Dominique Valbelle. "Komir. I. – The Discovery of Komir Temple. Preliminary Report. II. – Deux hymnes aux divinités de Komir : Anoukis et Nephthys." *BIFAO 83*. (1983), pp. 149-170.

- Favard-Meeks, Christine. <u>Le Temple de Behbeit el-Hagara: essai de reconstitution et d'interpretation</u>. Hamburg: Helmut Buske Verlag, 1991.

- Favard-Meeks, Christine. "Un temple d'Isis Reconstruire." *Archeologia 263*. 1990. 26-33.

- Favard-Meeks, Christine. "The Temple of Behbeit el-Hagara." <u>The Temple of Ancient Egypt: New Discoveries and Research</u>. Stephen Quirke (ed.), London: British Museum Press, 1997, pp. 102-111.

- Faulkner, R. O. <u>The Ancient Egyptian Pyramid Texts</u>. London: Oxford University Press, 1998.

- Faulkner, R. O<u>. The Ancient Egyptian Coffin Texts Vol 1-3</u>. Translated by R. O. Faulkner. England: Aris & Phillips, Ltd., 2004.

- Faulkner, R. O. <u>The Ancient Egyptian Book of the Dead</u>. Edited by Carol Andrews. Austin: University of Texas Press, 1985.

- Faulkner, R. O. and Ogden Goelet. <u>The Egyptian Book of the Dead: The Book of Going Forth By Day</u>. Chronicle Books, 1998.

- Faulkner, Raymond. <u>Concise Dictionary of Middle Egyptian</u>. London: Griffith Institute Oxford, 1972. Reprint, London: Butler and Tanner Ltd., 2002.

- Forrest, M. Isidora. Isis Magic: Cultivating a Relationship with the Goddess of Ten Thousand Names: Tenth Anniversary Edition (Revised and Expanded). Abiegnus House, 2013.
- Forrest, M. Isidora. Offering to Isis: Knowing the Goddess Through Her Sacred Symbols. St. Paul: Llewellyn Publications, 2005.
- Foster, John. Hymns, Prayers and Songs: An Anthology of Ancient Egyptian Lyric Poetry. Scholars Press, 1995.
- Frandsen, Paul John. "The Menstrual 'Taboo' in Ancient Egypt," in *The Journal of Near Eastern Studies, 66, no. 2*, (Univ. of Copenhagen, 2007), 81-105.
- Frandsen, Paul John. "Taboo," in Ancient Gods Speak: A Guide to Egyptian Religion. edited by Donald Redford. New York: Oxford University Press, 2002, pp. 349-351.
- Franke, Detlef. "Middle Kingdom Hymns and Other Sundry Religious Texts-An Inventory", in Egypt: Temple of the Whole World: Studies in Honour of Jan Assmann. Sibylle Meyer, ed. Brill Academic Publishers, 2004.
- Frankfurter, David. "Narrating Power: The Theory and Practice of the Magical Historiola in Ritual Spells," in Ancient Magic and Ritual Power. Brill Academic Publishers (2001), pp. 457-476.
- Frankfurter, David. Religion in Roman Egypt: Assimilation and Resistance. New Jersey: Princeton University Press, 1998.
- Gartland, Joan Wallace. "The Concept of Isis During the Egyptian Old Kingdom Based upon the Pyramid Texts". Dissertation: University of Chicago, IL 1968.
- Gasparro, Giulia Sfameni. "The Hellenistic Face of Isis: Cosmic and Saviour Goddess" in Nile into Tiber: Egypt in the Roman World: Proceedings of the IIIrd International Conference of Isis Studies, Leiden, May 11-14 2005. Laurent Bricault, Miguel John Versluys and Paul G. P. Meyboom, ed. Brill, 2007; pages 40-72.

- Goyon, Jean-Claude. Confirmation du Pouvoir Royal au Nouvel an : Brooklyn Museum papyrus 47.218.50. Institut Francais D'Archeologie Orientale et Brooklyn Museum, 1972.
- Goyon, Jean-Claude. "Inscriptions Tardives Du Temple de Mout à Karnak." *Journal of the American Research Center in Egypt.* Vol. 20, American Research Center in Egypt. (1983), pp. 47-61.
- Green, L. "Isis: The Egyptian Goddess who endured in the Graeco-Roman World." in *KMT: A Modern Journal of Ancient Egypt 5:4*, pages 60-68.
- Griffith, F. Ll. Catalogue of the Demotic Graffiti of the Dodecaschoenus. Oxford University Press, 1937.
- Griffith, F. Ll. Meroitic Inscriptions, Part II. Napata to Philae and Miscellaneous. London and Boston: Office of the Egypt Exploration Fund; 1862-1934.
- Griffith, F. Ll. Karanòg: The Meroitic Inscriptions of Shablûl and Karanòg. University Museum, 1911.
- Griffith, F. Ll. and Herbert Thompson, ed. The Leyden Papyrus: An Egyptian Magical Book. New York: Dover Publications, 1974.
- Griffith, F Ll. "Meroitic Studies" in *The Journal of Egyptian Archaeology, Vol. 3, No. 1 (Jan., 1916)*, pp. 22-30.
- Griffith, F. Ll. "Inscriptions," in El-Amrah and Abydos, 1899-1901. edited by David Randall-MacIver, Arthur Cruttenden Mace and Francis Llewellyn Griffith. Egyptian Exploration Fund, 1902.
- Griffiths, J. Gwyn. The Isis-Book: Metamorphosis XI. Brill Academic Publishers, 1997.
- Griffiths, J. Gwyn. "Isis." in Ancient Gods Speak: A Guide to Egyptian Religion. edited by Donald Redford. New York: Oxford University Press, 2002, pp. 169-172.

- Grimm, Alfred. Die Altägyptischen Festkalander in den Tempeln der griechisch-römischen Epoche. Harrassowitz, 1994.
- Hart, George. The Dictionary of Egyptian Gods and Goddesses. New York: Routledge and Kegan Paul Inc, 1986.
- Hart, George. The Legendary Past: Egyptian Myths. Austin: University of Texas Press, 1990.
- Hekster, Olivier. Rome and its Empire, AD 193-284. Edinburgh University Press, 2008.
- Herodotus. The Histories. translated by Aubrey de Selincourt. Penguin Classics, 1972.
- Heyob, Sharon Kelly. The Cult of Isis Among Women in the Greco-Roman World. Leiden: E. J. Brill, 1975.
- Hollis, Susan Tower. "Five Egyptian Goddesses in the Third Millennium BC: Neith, Hathor, Nut, Isis, Nephthys." in *KMT: A Modern Journal of Ancient Egypt*, 5:4. pp. 46-51 and 82-85.
- Houser-Wegner, Jennifer. "Wepwawet." in Ancient Gods Speak: A Guide to Egyptian Religion, ed. Donald Redford: New York: Oxford University Press, 2002, pp. 381-382.
- Hornung, Erik. Conceptions of God in Ancient Egypt: the One and the Many. Translated by John Baines. Ithaca: Cornell University Press, 1996.
- Hornung, Erik. Idea into Image: Essays on Ancient Egyptian Thought. Translated by Elizabeth Bredeck. New York: Princeton University Press, 1992.
- Illes, Judika. The Element Encyclopedia of 1000 Spells. Barnes and Noble, 2008.
- Jacq, Christian. Magic and Mystery in Ancient Egypt. Trans. By Janet M. Davis. Souvenir Press, 1998.
- Jacquet-Gordon, Helen. Temple of Khonsu, Volume 3. The Graffiti on the Khonsu Temple Roof at Karnak: A

Manifestation of Personal Piety. Oriental Institute of Chicago, 2003.

- Jones, M. and A. Milward. "Survey of the Temple of Isis Mistress of the Pyramid at Giza, 1980 Season: Main Temple Area," in *Journal of the Society for the Study of Egyptian Antiquity*. 12. (1982): 140-151.

- Junker, Hermann. Der Grosse Pylon des Tempels der Isis in Phila. Wien: Kommission bei Rudolf M. Rohrer, 1958.

- Junker, Hermann and Eric Winter. Das Geburtshaus des Tempels der Isis in Phila. Wien: Kommissionsverlag H. Böhlaus Nachf., 1965.

- Junker, Hermann. Das Gotterdekret: Uber das Abaton. Wien, 1913.

- Kahl, Jochem. Ancient Asyut: the First Synthesis after Three Hundred Years of Research. Harrassowitz Verlag, 2007.

- Kaldera, Raven and Kenaz Filan. Drawing Down the Spirits: Tradition and Technique of Spirit Possession. Destiny Books, 2009.

- Kaper, Olaf E. "Isis in Roman Dakhleh: Goddess of the Village, the Province and the Country," in Isis on the Nile: Egyptian Gods in Hellenistic and Roman Egypt: Proceedings of the IVth International Conference of Isis Studies, Liege, November 27-29, 2008. Bricault, Laurent and Miguel John Versluys, ed. (Brill Academic Pub, 2010), pp. 149-180.

- Kinsley, David. "Isis, Heavenly Queen," in The Goddesses' Mirror: Visions of the Divine from East to West. New York: State University of New York Press, 1989.

- Kitchen, Kenneth Anderson. Ramesside Inscriptions: Merenptah and the Late Nineteenth Dynasty: Volume IV. Blackwell Publishing, 2003.

- Kockelmann, Holger. Praising the Goddess: A Comparative and Annotated Re-Edition of Six Demotic Hymns and Praises Addressed to Isis. New York: Walter de Gruyter, 2008.

- Kruchten, Jean-Marie. "Oracles," in Ancient Gods Speak: A Guide to Egyptian Religion. edited by Donald Redford. New York: Oxford University Press, 2002, pp. 298-302.
- Kurth, Dieter. Die Inschriften des Tempels von Edfu. Abteilung I Übersetzungen; Band 1. Edfou VIII. Harrassowitz Verlag, 1998.
- Leitz, Christian, ed. Lexicon der Aegyptischen Goetter und Goetterbezeichnungen (LAGG, OLA 110, Band 1). Peeters, 2002.
- Lesko, Barbara. The Great Goddesses of Egypt. Oklahoma: University of Oklahoma Press, 1999.
- Lesko, Leonard H, ed. Pharaoh's Workers: The Village of Deir El Medina. Ithaca: Cornell University Press, 1994.
- Levai, Jessica. Aspects of the Goddess Nephthys, Especially During the Greaco-Roman Period in Egypt. Rhode Island: Brown University Dissertation, 2007.
- Lewis, H. Jeremiah. The Balance of the Two Lands: Writings on Greco-Egyptian Polytheism. Nysa Press, 2009.
- Lichtheim, Miriam. Ancient Egyptian Literature Vol 1: The Old and Middle Kingdoms. Los Angeles: University of California Press, 1973.
- Lichtheim, Miriam. Ancient Egyptian Literature Vol 2: The New Kingdom. Los Angeles: University of California Press, 1976.
- Lichtheim, Miriam. Ancient Egyptian Literature Vol 3: The Late Period. Los Angeles: University of California Press, 1980.
- Lippert, Sandra. Tebtynis und Soknopaiu Nesos. Leben im römerzeitlichen Fajum. Harrassowitz Verlag, 2005.
- Loewe, Micheal and Carmen Blacker, ed. Oracles and Divination. Colorado: Shambhala Publications, 1981.

- Lurker, Manfred. An Illustrated Dictionary of The Gods and Symbols of Ancient Egypt. London: Thames and Hudson, 1980.
- MacQuitty, William. Island of Isis: Philae, Temple of the Nile. New York: Charles Scribner's Sons, 1976.
- Mair, Melissa. "The Transformation of a Goddess: Depictions of Isis throughout the Ancient Mediterranean World." Dissertation: Emory University, 2012.
- Manniche, Lise. An Ancient Egyptian Herbal. Austin: University of Texas Press, 1989.
- Mariette, Auguste. Denderah: Description Generale du Grand Temple de Cette Ville. Volume 1-6. Paris: Libraire a France, 1870.
- Meeks, Dimitri and Christine Farvard-Meeks. Daily Life of the Egyptian Gods. Translated by G. M. Goshgarian. Ithaca: Cornell University Press, 1996.
- Meyer, Marvin and Richard Smith, ed. Ancient Christian Magic: Coptic Texts of Ritual Power. HarperSanFrancisco, 1994 ; Princeton University Press, 1999.
- Mills, A.J. "Two Sekhmet Statues at Trewithen in Cornwall". The Journal of Egyptian Archaeology 65, 1979, p 166.
- Morenz, Seigfried. Egyptian Religion. Translated by Ann E. Keep. Ithaca: Cornell Paperbacks, 1996.
- Morgan, Mogg. The Wheel of the Year in Ancient Egypt. Mandrake of Oxford, 2011.
- Moyer, Ian S. Isidorus at the Gates of the Temple. University of Chicago, 2010. Online PDF found here: http://lucian.uchicago.edu/blogs/csar/files/2010/03/Moyer-Isidorus-at-the-Gates-of-the-Temple.pdf
- Muller, Maya. "Re and Re-Horakhty," in Ancient Gods Speak: A Guide to Egyptian Religion. edited by Donald Redford. New York: Oxford University Press, 2002, pp.325-328.

- Münster, Maria. <u>Untersuchungen zur Göttin Isis vom Alten Reich bis zum Ende des Neuen Reiches</u>. Munchner Ägyptologische Studien 11. Berlin: Verlag Bruno Hessling, 1968.
- Murray, Margaret Alice and Joseph Grafton Milne, Walter Ewing Crum. <u>The Osireion at Abydos</u>. Gilbert and Rivington, LtD, 1904.
- Murray, Margaret. <u>Egyptian Religious Poetry</u>. John Murray Publishers, 1949.
- Mysliwiec, Karol. <u>Eighteenth Dynasty Before the Amarna Period</u>. E. J. Brill Leiden. 1985.
- Naville, Édouard Henri and Francis Llewellyn Griffith, et al. <u>Ahnas el Medineh: The Tomb of Paheri at El Kab</u>. Egyptian Exploration Fund, 1894.
- Naydler, Jeremy. <u>Temple of the Cosmos: The Ancient Egyptian Experience of the Sacred</u>. Vermont: Inner Traditions International, 1996.
- Naydler, Jeremy. <u>The Shamanic Wisdom in the Pyramid Texts: The Mystical Tradition of Ancient Egypt</u>. Vermont: Inner Traditions International, 2005.
- Nicoll, Kiya. <u>The Traveller's Guide to the Duat</u>. Megalithica Books, 2012.
- O'Connor, David. <u>Abydos: The First Pharoahs and the Cult of Osiris</u>. Thames and Hudson, 2011.
- Nelson, Harold H. "The Calendar of Feasts and Offerings at Medinet Habu." <u>Work in Western Thebes 1931-33</u>. Harold H. Nelson and Uvo Holscher, ed. Oriental Institute of the University of Chicago Press, 1934, pp. 1-52.
- Pantalacci, Laure and Claude Traunecker. <u>Le Temple d'El-Qal'a. Vol. I</u>. Institut Francais d'Archeologie Orientale, 1990.
- Pantalacci, Laure and Claude Traunecker. <u>Le Temple d'El-Qal'a. Vol. II</u>. Institut Francais d'Archeologie Orientale, 1998.

- Parker, Richard. The Calendars of Ancient Egypt. (The Oriental Institute of the University of Chicago. Studies in ancient oriental civilization). University of Chicago Press, 1950.
- Pausanias. Description of Greece: Books 1-2. translated by W. H. S. Jones. (Loeb Classical Library, 1918; Harvard University Press, reprint.
- Perpillou-Thomas, Francoise. Fêtes d'Egypte ptolémaïque et romaine, d'après la documentation papyrologique grecque. (Studia Hellenistica Series 31). Peeters Publishers, 1993.
- Peters-Desteract, Madeleine. Philae: Le Domaine d'Isis. Champollion. Monaco: Editions du rocher, 1997.
- Piankoff, Alexandre. Mythological Papyri: Bollingen III Series. University of Princeton Press, 1957.
- Piankoff, Alexandre. The Shrines of Tut-Ankh-Amun: Bollingen II. University of Princeton Press, 1955.
- Piankoff, Alexandre. Tomb of Ramesses VI: Bollingen I. University of Princeton Press, 1954.
- Pinch, Geraldine. Magic in Ancient Egypt. Austin: University of Texas Press, 1995.
- Pinch, Geraldine. Egyptian Mythology: A Guide to the Gods, Goddesses and Traditions of Ancient Egypt. New York: Oxford University Press, 2004.
- Pinch, Geraldine. "Offerings to Hathor," Folklore Vol. 93, No. 2. (1982), pp. 138-150.
- Plutarch. On Isis and Osiris. Archeon Press, 2012.
- Poo, Mu-Chou. Wine and Wine Offering in the Religion of Ancient Egypt. New York: Kegan Paul International, 1995.
- Poo, Mu-chou, 2010, "Liquids in Temple Ritual". Willeke Wendrich (ed.), UCLA Encyclopedia of Egyptology, Los Angeles. http://digital2.library.ucla.edu/viewItem.do?ark=21198/zz002 5dxbr

- Quirke, Stephen. The Cult of Ra: Sun-Worship in Ancient Egypt. New York: Thames and Hudson, 2001.
- Quirke, Stephen G. J. "Judgement of the Dead." in Ancient Gods Speak: A Guide to Egyptian Religion. edited by Donald Redford. New York: Oxford University Press, 2002, pp.173-178.
- Ray, J. D. Demotic Papyri and Ostraca from Qasr Ibrim. Egypt Exploration Society, 2005.
- Ray, J. D. "A Pious Soldier: Stele Aswan 1057". *The Journal of Egyptian Archaeology*, Vol. 73 (1987), pp. 169-180.
- Redford, Donald, ed. Ancient Gods Speak: A Guide to Egyptian Religion. New York: Oxford University Press, 2002.
- Reidy, Richard. Eternal Egypt: Ancient Rituals for the Modern World. iUniverse, 2010.
- Regula, deTraci. The Mysteries of Isis: Her Worship and Magick. Llewellyn Publications, 1995.
- Ritner, Robert Kriech. The Mechanics of Ancient Egyptian Magical Practice. Chicago: Oriental Institute of the University of Chicago, Studies in Ancient Oriental Civilization #54, 1993.
- Ritner, Robert K. "Anubis and the Lunar Disc," in *The Journal of Egyptian Archaeology, Vol. 71 (1985)*, pp. 149-155.
- Ritner, Robert. "The Legend of Isis and the Name of Re (I.22): D. Turin 1993" in William W. Hallo (ed.), The Context of Scripture, Vol. I. (Brill 1997), pages 33-34.
- Roberts, Alison. Hathor Rising: The Power of the Goddess in Ancient Egypt. Vermont: Inner Traditions International, 1997.
- Roberts, Alison. My Heart My Mother: Death and Rebirth in Ancient Egypt. England: Northgate Publishers, 2000.
- Roberts, Alison. Goddess Shrine, Goddess Queen: Egypt's Anointing Mysteries. Northgate Publishers, 2008.

- Rose, Pamela J., et al. The Meroitic Temple Complex of Qasr Ibrim. London: Egypt Exploration Society, 2007.
- Roth, Ann Macy and Catherine H. Roehrig. "Magical Bricks and the Bricks of Birth," *The Journal of Egyptian Archaeology*, Vol. 88 (2002), pp. 121-139.
- Rowlandson, Jane. Women and Society in Greek and Roman Egypt: A Sourcebook. Cambridge University Press, 1998.
- Rutherford, Ian. "Island of the Extremity: Space, Language and Power in the Pilgrimage Traditions of Philae." in Pilgrimage and Holy Space in Late Antique Egypt, edited by David Frankfurter. Leiden; Boston: Brill, 1998, pp. 229-56.
- Salzman, Michele Renee. On Roman Time: The Codex Calendar of 354 and the Rhythms of Urban Life in Late Antiquity. University of California Press, 1990.
- Sauneron, Serge. The Priests of Ancient Egypt. Translated by David Lorton. Ithaca: Cornell University Press, 2000.
- Sauneron, Serge. Esna V: Les fetes religieuses d'esna aux derniers siecles du paganisme. Institut français d'archéologie orientale, 2004.
- Scott, Nora E. "Metternich Stela," *The Metropolitan Museum of Art Bulletin*, New Series, Vol. 9, No. 8 (Apr., 1951), 201-217.
- Schott, Siegfried. "Feasts of Thebes." Work in Western Thebes 1931-33. Harold H. Nelson and Uvo Holscher, ed. Oriental Institute of the University of Chicago Press, 1934, pp. 63-90.
- Shafer, Byron, ed. Religion in Ancient Egypt: Gods, Myths and Personal Practice. Ithaca: Cornell University Press, 1991.
- Shennum, David. English-Egyptian Index of Faulkner's Concise Dictionary of Middle Egyptian. Malibu: Undena Publications, 1977.
- Simon, Catherine. "Geb." in Ancient Gods Speak: A Guide to Egyptian Religion. Donald Redford, ed. New York: Oxford University Press, 2002, pp. 298.

- Siuda-Legan, Tamara. The Neteru of Kemet. Eschaton Productions, 1994.

- Siuda, Tamara. Nebt-Het: Lady of the House. Illinois: Stargazer Design, 2010.

- Siuda, Tamara. The Ancient Egyptian Prayerbook. Illinois: Stargazer Design, 2009.

- Solmsen, Friedrich. Isis among the Greeks and Romans. Cambridge: Harvard University Press, 1979.

- Spalinger, Anthony. Three Studies on Egyptian Feasts and Their Chronological Implications. Maryland: Halgo, 1992.

- Spalinger, Anthony. "Some Remarks on the Epagomenal Days in Ancient Egypt." *Journal of Near Eastern Studies*, Vol. 54, No. 1, (Jan., 1995), pp. 33-47.

- Steindorff, George and Emma J. Edelstein. "Reliefs from the Temples of Sebennytos and Iseion in American Collections." *The Journal of the Walters Art Gallery*, Vol. 7/8, (1944/1945), pp. 38-59.

- Stadler, Martin Andreas. "Der Isishymnus E.14 aus dem Isistempel von Assuan" in The *Journal of Egyptian Archaeology* (*JEA*). *Volume 98*, (2012), pp. 291-297.

- Strandberg, Asa. The Gazelle in Ancient Egyptian Art: Image and Meaning. Uppsala Universitet, 2009.

- Thomas, Susanna. "A Saite Figure of Isis in the Petrie Museum" in *The Journal of Egyptian Archaeology*, Vol. 85, (1999), pp. 232-235.

- Traunecker, C. Coptos: Hommes et Dieux Sur le Parvis de Geb. Peeters, 1992.

- Vanderlip, Vera Frederika. The Four Greek Hymns of Isidorus and the Cult of Isis. Canada: A. K. Hakkert, 1972.

- Vandier, Jacques. Le Papyrus Jumilhac. Paris: Musée du Louvre. 1961.

- Vassilika, Eleni. Ptolemaic Philae. Peeters, 1989.

- Te Velde, Herman. **"Towards a Minimal Definition of the Goddess Mut,"** in *Jaarbericht van het Vooraziatisch-Egyptisch Genootschap Ex Oriente Lux. Vol. 26.* **(1979-1980), 3-9.**

- te Velde, Herman. "Mut, the Eye of Re." in S. Schoske (ed). Akten des vierten Internationalen Ägyptologen-Kongresses München vol. 3 (1985), (Studien zur Altägyptischen Kultur Beihefte 3), pp 395-403.

- Te Velde, H. "The Cat as Sacred Animal of the Goddess Mut." In M. Heerma van Voss et al (eds). *Studies in Egyptian Religion.* Leiden, E.J. Brill, 1982.

- Tripani, Luigi and Amentet Neferet. Egyptian Religious Calendar: CDXV-CDXVI Great Year of Ra (2015 CE). Amentet Neferet, 2014.

- Troy, Lana. "Mut Enthroned," in Essays on ancient Egypt: in honour of Herman te Velde . J. Vandijk, ed. Brill Academic Pub, 1997), pp. 301-316.

- Tyldesley, Joyce. The Penguin Book of Myths and Legends of Ancient Egypt. Penguin Books, 2011.

- von Lieven, Alexandra. "Der Isishymnus Deir Chelouit 154, 1-10." *Acta Antiqua: Volume 46, Numbers 1-2/March 2006.* Akadémiai Kiadó, 165-171.

- Watterson, Barbara. The House of Horus at Edfu: Ritual in an Ancient Egyptian Temple. Great Britian: Tempus Publishing Limited, 1998.

- Widmer, Ghislaine. "On Egyptian Religion at Soknopaiou Nesos in the Roman Period," in Tebtynis und Soknopaiu Nesos. Leben im römerzeitlichen Fajum. Sandra Lippert. Harrassowitz Verlag, 2005, pp. 171-184.

- Wild, Robert A. Water in the Cultic Worship of Isis and Sarapis. Brill Academic Publishers, 1981.

- Wilkinson, Richard H. The Complete Gods and Goddesses of Ancient Egypt. New York: Thames and Hudson, 2003.

- Wilkinson, Richard H. The Complete Temples of Ancient Egypt. New York: Thames and Hudson, 2000.
- Wilkinson, Richard H. Reading Egyptian Art. New York: Thames and Hudson, 1992.
- Wilkinson, Richard H. Symbol and Magic in Egyptian Art. New York: Thames and Hudson, 1994.
- Wilkinson, John Gardner. The Ancient Egyptians. New York: Crescent Books, 1988.
- Willems, Harco, and Filip Coppens, Marleen De Meyer and Peter Dils. The Temple of Shanhur: Volume 1. Peeters, 2003.
- Wilson, J. A. "The Theban Tomb (No. 409) of Si-Mut, Called Kiki," in *Journal of Near Eastern Studies vol 29* (1970), pp. 187-192.
- Winlock, Herbert Eustis. The Temple of Ramesses 1 at Abydos. Arno Press, 1973.
- Wisner, Kerry. Eye of the Sun: The Sacred Legacy of Ancient Egypt. Kephra Publications, 2011.
- Wisner, Kerry. Song of Hathor: Ancient Egyptian Ritual for Today. Kephra Publications, 2011.
- Wisner, Kerry. Pillar of Ra: Ancient Egyptian Festivals for Today. Kephra Publications, 2011.
- Witt, Reginald Eldred. Isis in the Ancient World. Baltimore: Johns Hopkins University Press, 1997.
- Yellin, Janice. "Abaton-Style Milk Libations at Meroe." Meroitica: Schriften zur altsudanesischen Geschichte und Archaologie. 6 (1982): 151-155.
- Zabkar, Louis V. Hymns to Isis in Her Temple at Philae. London: University Press of New England, 1988.
- Zabkar, Louis V. "Adaptation of the Ancient Egyptian Texts to the Temple Ritual at Philae". *The Journal of Egyptian Archaeology* Vol. 66 (1980), pp. 127-136.

- Zabkar, L. V. "Six Hymns to Isis in the Sanctuary of Her Temple at Philae and Their Theological Significance. Part I". *The Journal of Egyptian Archaeology*, Vol. 69, (1983), pp. 115-137.
- Zecchi, Marco. "Osiris in the Fayyum." Fayyum Studies: Volume 2. Sergio Pernigotti and Marco Zecchi, ed. (Ante Quem and Dipartimento di Archeologia dell'Università di Bologna, 2006), pp. 117-145.
- **Zivie, Christiane M**. Le Temple de Deir el Chelouit, 1: 1-55, Inscriptions du propylône et de la porte du temple. Cairo: IFAO, 1982.
- **Zivie, Christiane M**. Le Temple de Deir el Chelouit, 2: 56-89, Inscriptions du pronaos. Cairo: IFAO, 1983.
- **Zivie, Christiane M**. Le Temple de Deir el Chelouit, 3: 90-157: Inscriptions du naos. Cairo: IFAO, 1986.
- **Zivie-Coche, Christiane M.** Giza au Primier Millenaire: Autour du Temple d'Isis Dame des Pyramides. Museum of Fine Arts Boston, 1991.

Glossary

- Abu: (Greek: Elephantine) Khnum's sacred city on the First Cataract of the Nile.
- Abdju: (Modern: Abydos) This is the sacred city of Wesir and the place of the burial site of the first ancient Egyptian kings.
- Akh (s)/Akhu (p): the ancestors, beloved dead,
- Alexandria: A metropolitan port city in the Ptolemaic period where Aset (Isis) was honored in the Lighthouse of Alexandria on Pharos Island.
- Amenti: This is an alternative name for the Duat. The name comes from the goddess Amentet, the Lady of the West. She is the goddess of the sunset, the night sky, the deceased and the unseen realm. Amenti is a title and manifestation of the goddesses Aset, Hethert, Nebet Het and Nut.
- Amun-Ra: a syncretic deity who rose to prominence in the New Kingdom. He was a combination of Amun and Ra. He is the husband of Mut and father of Khonsu.
- Anuket: (Greek: Anukis) She is a goddess who is associated with the Nile's inundation and whose sacred animal is the gazelle. Anuket was associated with the Nile as the waters receded while Satet was associated with the Nile as the waters rose. She was worshiped at Elephantine along with Satet and Khnum and at Komir she shared a temple with Nebet Het.
- Aset: (also Auset; Greek: Isis)-a goddess of authority, sovereignty and kings. She is the goddess of magic par excellence who owns Ra's Name. She is a solar Eye of Ra who wards off enemies from her husband, son and the sun god. On the Night Boat, Aset wards off Apep with her magic. She

heralds the New Year rising in the sky as the star Sopdet. She is the wife of Wesir and the mother of Heru-sa-Aset.

- Atinoe: (Greek: Antinopolis) Ancient city dedicated to the Antinious, the deified lover of Emperor Hadrian who drowned in the Nile.

- Ba (s)/Bau (p): The eternal essence of a being, the soul. The *ba* of a deity went into the cult statues and other theophanies were the manifestations of the deity on earth. A physical manifestation of a deity such as a cult statue, an animal or a natural force. The *ba* of a human is an eternal part of the soul.

- Bast: (Greek: Bastet) a lioness goddess who protects her father Ra, is an avenging Eye of Ra and is a goddess of the yearly solar cycle. She is also a goddess of joy and music like Hethert. In later periods, she became associated with the more domestic housecat.

- Behdet: (Greek: Apollonopolis Magna; Modern: Edfu) The city and temple are sacred to Heru Wer or Horus the Elder.

- Djedet: (Greek: Mendes) This city was sacred to the fish goddess Hatmehyt and her consort, Banebdjedet.

- Djehuty: (Greek: Thoth) This is the ibis or baboon headed god of time, wisdom, math, science, scribes, recordkeeping and the moon. In some inscriptions, Djehuty is the father or son of Aset.

- Dua: an ancient Egyptian word meaning praise, worship or adoration. It can be used as an exclamation meaning to praise or glorify a god or goddess.

- Duat: This word means the sunrise and sunset. This word is translated as the "Underworld". This is the Unseen Realm where the gods and the dead reside. Another name for this place is Amenti.

- Geb: the earth god who was associated with the land itself and all that grows upon it. He is associated with all the minerals in the earth. He is associated with the dead since the dead are buried in the earth. In the beginning, he was separated from his wife, Nut so that the earth and sky could be created. He is the father of Aset, Nebet Het, Set, Wesir and Heru Wer.

- Gebtu: (Greek: Koptos or Coptos; Modern: Qift) a sacred town to Min, Aset, Wesir and Heru-sa-Aset.
- Hebyt: (also Per-Hebitet; Greek: Isiopolis; currently Behbeit el-Hagar) An ancient sacred city to Aset. The ancient Egyptian name of this city means "House of the Festive Goddess". Her temple in this city is called the Iseion or Temple of Isis in Greek.
- Heka: (literally, "magic"). This is a god and a concept. The concept is a force of energy that resides in all things. It can be manipulated by deities and humans. It has been translated as magic, but it is really the power of the ka (life force) in motion.
- Hekau: a magician, a sorcerer or sorceress, one who uses heka, a plural form of "magic"
- Henu: a ritual gesture where one's arms are outstretched, parallel to the shoulders, with palms facing outward and slightly cupped, toward the image of the deity. When this gesture is complete, then one would do a full prostration before the image of the god or goddess.
- Heru pa Khered: (Greek: Harpokrates; Horus the Child) a form of Heru-sa-Aset who is a child. He and his mother are mentioned together in many healing spells.
- Heru nedj itef: (Greek: Harendotes; Horus, Savior of His Father) The form of Heru-sa-Aset who has battled Set and won the throne of Egypt. He has inherited the throne of his father.
- Heru-sa-Aset: (Greek: Harsiese; Horus son of Isis)-The son of Aset and Wesir who can manifest in many forms such as a child, a warrior battling Set for the throne and a triumphant King. He is the god of kingship and proficient in magical spells because of his mother. He is a god of strength,

leadership and community. He is often portrayed as a hawk headed god with the Double Crown.

- Heru-sema-tawy: (Greek: Harsomtus; Horus the Uniter of the Two Lands) A form of Heru the Child who is the son of Hethert and Heru Wer.

- Heru Wer: (Greek: Haroeris; Horus the Elder) the sky god of kings, and communities whose eyes are the sun and the moon. He is a protector and a warrior. He is the twin brother of Set, uncle of Heru-sa-Aset and the brother of Aset, Wesir and Nebet Het. He is often portrayed as a falcon headed god with the White Crown.

- Hethert: (also Hetharu; Greek: Hathor) a joyous goddess of beauty, love, and fertility. She is an Eye of Ra and an avenging solar deity. She is also a goddess who protects the dead.

- Het-Ka-Ptah: (also Mennefer; Memphis) The sacred city to the craftsmen god Ptah. The name means "House of the Ka of Ptah".

- Hypostasis: a distinct, seperate aspect within a unified god

- Imet: (currently known as Tell Nabasha) A city that was sacred to Wadjet.

- Iunet: (currently known as Dendera) This is the sacred city of the goddess Hethert.

- Iunu: (also On; Greek: Heliopolis) This the sacred city of Ra and the gods of his creation myth. The Ennead of this city consisted of Ra, Shu, Tefnut, Nut, Geb, Wesir, Aset, Nebet Het, Set and Heru Wer.

- Ka (s)/Kau (p): the vital essence of a person or deity; the collective vital essence of a family line or kingly lineage

- Khent-min: (also Ipu or Apu; Greek: Chemmis or Panopolis; currently Akhmim) A city sacred to Min. In the Wesir Mythos, Aset takes her son to the marshes here to raise her son.

- Khmun (Greek: Hermopolis) This is the sacred city of Djehuty.

- Khnum: a Ram-headed god of the Nile's inundation, potters and a master craftsman. He creates the kau of humans on his potter's wheel. Khnum is also one of the creators of the world.
- Ma'at: (Greek: Mayet)-a goddess and a concept of truth, order and balance of the universe.
- Menat: (also Menet) a necklace used like a rattle in ritual. It is especially used for the goddesses.
- Mehet Weret: (also Celestial Cow; Greek: Methyer) This is the cow goddess of the primeval waters, creation, the birth of the sun god and the heavenly sky. She is the caretaker of the dead since the stars fill the night sky. She is a manifestation of Nut, Nit, Nebet Het, Hethert and Aset.
- Min: the ithyphallic god of fertility and procreation. Aset can be paired with him as her consort or her son.
- Mut: a goddess of sovereignty, royalty and an Eye of Ra. The wife of Amun-Ra and mother of Khonsu.
- Nebet Het: (Greek: Nephthys)-Her name can mean Lady of the House, Lady of the Temple or Lady of the Tomb. She is a goddess who protects boundaries such as the sacred from the profane or twilight lands during dawn and dusk. As a solar goddess, she is an Eye of Ra and is a protector of Ra and Wesir. She weeps with Aset causing the flooding of the Nile. In some myths, Yinepu is her son. She can be a consort of Set, Ra or Wesir.
- Nefertem: (also Nefertum) A patron god of scents and fragrances, Nefertem is a god associated with the lotus and wears on upon his head. He also cen be depicted as a child sitting on a lotus flower. He wards off evil in his leonine form. He is the son of Sekhmet and Ptah. He is also considered the son of Bast.
- Nekheb: (currently known as El-Kab) This is the sacred city of the vulture goddess Nekhbet.

- Nekhen: (Greek: Hierakonpolis) This city is sacred to Heru of Nekhen, the god Khnum and the goddess Nit.

- Nit: (Greek: Neith) The tutelary goddess of Lower Egypt. She wears the red crown and holds bows and arrows. She is a primordial goddess who began creation. She has a manifestation as the celestial cow where she is a creator deity, the lady of the primeval ocean and the night sky, holding the dead. She is a goddess associated with protection of the dead as she protects one of the canopic jars. She is a mother of Sobek and a consort of Set.

- Nut: The goddess of the night sky filled with stars. She is the goddess of the dead as their mother and caretaker. She gives birth to the sun god each morning and devours him each evening. As the celestial cow, she is the goddess of the primeval waters and the dead. She is the mother of Aset, Nebet Het, Set, Wesir and Heru Wer.

- Of Iunu: (Greek: Heliopolitaine; of Heliopolis) This is normally translated as the Heliopolitaine or the one of Heliopolis or the city of Iunu in Ancient Egyptian.

- Per Bast: (Greek: Bubastis) This is the sacred city of the goddess Bast.

- Per Hethert: (also Tpyhwt; Greek: Aphroditopolis; Modern: Atfih) A city sacred to Hethert.

- Per Medjed: (Greek: Oxyrhynchus) This city was sacred to Wepwawet during the New Kingdom (along with Aset and Hethert).

- Per Wesir: (also Djedu; Greek: Busiris) This city was sacred to Wesir.

- Pesdjet: (Greek: Ennead) a group of important deities of cities; this number could be nine deities, but it was not limited to that number.

- Pharos Island: A small island in the city of Alexandria where a Lighthouse once stood as one of the Seven Wonders of the

World. Aset of Pharos (Isis Pharia) was honored here as its patron goddess.

- Pilak: (also P'aaleq; Greek: Philae) The sacred temple and island to Aset during the Late through the Roman periods of ancient Egyptian history. The temple was relocated to Agilkia Island due to the construction of the Aswan Dam.

- Ptah: A creator god of Memphis who is the divine patron of craftsmen. He is the consort of Sekhmet and father of Nefertem.

- Ra: (also Re)-He is the sun god who created the world and who rules among the gods as their King. He is the father of many gods and goddesses, including Aset. Ra is one of the gods associated with kingship and he is often portrayed as a man with the head of a hawk wearing a solar disk.

- Ra Heruakhety: (Greek: Ra Horakhty; Ra-Horus of the Two Horizons) A fusion of the sun god Ra and Heru Wer. He represents the sun's journey both by day and night. He is often portrayed as a man with a falcon's head with a solar disk for his crown.

- Renenutet: (Greek: Thermuthis or Hermouthis) A cobra-headed goddess of the harvest and the protection of granaries. She is a goddess associated with fate and childbirth. She is a protective Eye of Ra goddess who destroys enemies. She is the consort of either Sobek or Geb. She is the mother of Nehebkau.

- Satet: (Greek: Satis) a tutelary goddess of Elephantine and the Nile's waters. She wears the White Crown encased in antelope horns. Her consort is Khnum and her daughter is Anuket. She can be syncretized with Aset.

- Shedet: (Greek: Crocodilopolis; Modern: Dime or Faiyum) The marshes sacred to the crocodile god Sobek. Aset, Wesir and Heru-sa-Aset were worshipped alongside Sobek in this nome during the Middle Kingdom through the Roman period.

- Shu: The primordial god of air and sunlight. He is the consort of Tefnut and father of Nut and Geb. He is often portrayed as a man wearing an ostrich feathered headdress or in leonine form.

- Sekhmet: (Greek: Sachmis)-a lioness-headed goddess who is the patron of healing and illness using magic and medicine to cure disease. As a daughter of Ra, she protects her Father from evil forces. Like many goddesses, she is an Eye of Ra. She is a protector and a warrior who defends ma'at. She is the patron of healers and surgeons. She is the mother of Nefertem and her consort is the creator god Ptah.

- Senem: (Greek: Abaton; currently Bigeh) The island is nearby the Temple of Philae. A temple to Wesir was on that island where Aset would honor her husband during weekly processions.

- Serqet: (also Selket; Greek: Selkis)-a scorpion goddess known for her healing abilities;

- Seshat: She is the goddess of writing, scribes record-keeping and recording the lives of kings. She was the patron of the "stretching the cord" ritual before a temple was built. As the tutelary goddess of scribes, she is often depicted holding scribe implements. She is often depicted wearing a leopard skin over her attire and her head is adorned with a seven pointed palmette with a two bovine horns pointing downward.

- Set: (also Seth)-He is the god of storms, the desert, foreigners, outsiders and strength. He guarded Ra's bark and killed Apep. In some myths, he is also the one who slays Wesir and challenges Heru-sa-Aset for the throne.

- Shai: (Greek: Psais; Agathos Daimon) The god of fate, fortune and destiny

- Sobek: (Greek: Suchos)-the crocodile god of the Nile waters, protection, strength and the sun. In some locations such as the Faiyum, Sobek is the son of Aset and Wesir.

- Sopdet: (Greek: Sothis; today known as Sirius)-a form of Aset who brings the Nile's inundation and heralds the New Year as She rises in the sky. As the star Sopdet, Aset follows Wesir (Orion) in the sky.

- Swenett: (Greek: Syene; Modern: Aswan or Assuan) A trade-city nearby Philae sacred to the goddess that the city was named for.

- Syncretic Deities: two deities who have fused to make a third, separate deity which still contains the uniqueness of the two deities such as Aset-Tayet, Aset-Nut and Aset-Mut.

- Tayet: (also Tait)-a deity of purification and the linen wrappings of the dead. She can be syncretized or considered an aspect of Aset.

- Ta-senet (also Iunyt; Greek: Latopolis or Letopolis; Modern: Esna) This city is sacred to the god Khnum and Nit.

- Tefnut: a lioness goddess who is an Eye of Ra and a lady of moisture. She is a primordial deity as she was the first goddess Ra created. She is the mother of Nut and the grandmother of Aset and her siblings.

- Tjebu: (Greek: Antinopolis) The city was sacred to Set.

- Uraeus: the fiery cobra who protects the sun god. Whose solar power is destructive toward enemies and protective for everyone else. All goddesses (and a few gods) with the epithet Eye of Ra are associated with this cobra.

- Wadjet: (Greek: Buto) The patron goddess of Lower Egypt. She is depicted as a Uraeus and can also be depicted as a cobra headed woman. She is associated with royalty and protection. She is also an Eye of Ra.

- Waset: (Greek: Thebes) The sacred city of Amun, Mut and Khonsu during the New Kingdom and beyond.

- Wepwawet: (also, Upuaut; Greek: Ophois) a Jackal god who is the Opener of the Way; he paves the way for armies, childbirth, the sun to rise, rituals to the gods and for the dead to cross over. He is associated with the wolf by the Greeks. He is a son of Aset.
- Wesir: (Greek: Osiris)-the god of vegetation and the king of the afterlife. Aset and Nebet Het mourn him after he is slain by Set. In some myths, he drowns in the Nile. Aset and Nebet Het search for him, find his body and bury it. Wesir is the father of Heru-sa-Aset.
- Yinepu: (Greek: Anubis) the Jackal-headed god of embalming, a psychopomp for the deceased and a guardian of tombs. Depending on the myth, the son or adopted son of Aset.
- Zau: (Greek: Sais) The sacred city of the goddess Nit.
- Zawty: (Greek: Lykopolis; currently known as Asyut) This is the sacred city to Wepwawet.

Other Books by
Chelsea Luellon Bolton

Lady of Praise, Lady of Power: Ancient Hymns of the Goddess Aset

Printed in Great Britain
by Amazon